Legends of
FOOTBALL

GRAHAM**BETTS**

Legends of
FOOTBALL

This revised edition first published in the UK in 2007

© Green Umbrella Publishing 2007

Printed and bound in China

ISBN: 978-1-905828-33-3

CONTENTS

Legends of
FOOTBALL

CARLOS**ALBERTO**

Captain of the Brazilian side when they won the World Cup for a third time in 1970, Carlos Alberto Torres may not have had the same kind of profile as some of his team-mates, but it is certain they could not have won the World Cup without his steadying influence.

Born in Rio de Janeiro, Carlos signed with the Fluminense club as a professional in 1963, but it was a move to Santos three years later, where he first linked with Pelé at club level, that saw him establish himself as a leading defender. In the space of a little over ten years, Carlos helped the club win a total of eight major national and regional titles, an impressive tally. Like Pelé, Carlos also rejected overtures from a number of European clubs, preferring to ply his trade in South America whilst he was at the peak of his career, an admirable decision.

He did however return to Fluminense in 1974 and was instrumental in the club winning two consecutive Campeonato Carioca championships during his three years with the club. A move to Fluminense's bitter rivals Flamengo followed in 1977, but this was a short-lived move that subsequently saw Carlos linking once again with Pelé, this time in the North American Soccer League with Cosmos. Whilst Pelé provided most of the glamour at Cosmos, it was Carlos Alberto who was the rock upon which Cosmos built a championship-winning side in 1977 and 1978. Carlos then headed to the west coast to play for California Surf for a season, returning to Cosmos in 1982 and helping them to the title again, Carlos's third such medal from the NASL. It was fitting that he should then play a farewell match in September 1982, a match between Cosmos and former club Flamengo in New York.

It is, of course, as captain of the Brazilians that Carlos made his worldwide reputation. There was no doubting the flair of the 1970 side, with the likes of Pelé, Jairzinho and Gerson providing most of the goals and the action, but at a time when Brazil was not particularly noted for the abilities of their defenders, Carlos Alberto was the exception. Tough in the tackle and visionary when it came to distributing the ball, Carlos also made the occasional foray upfield when the opportunity arose and scored one of the goals of the

Born: Rio de Janeiro, 17th July 1944
Debut: Brazil v England, 30/5/1964
Appearances: 53 caps for Brazil
Honours: World Cup winner (1970), Brasileiro Champion (1965, 1968), Campeao Torneio Rio Sao Paulo (1966), Paulista Champion (1965, 1967, 1968, 1969, 1973), Champion Recopa Sul Americano (1968), Champion Recopa Mundial (1968), NASL Champion (1977, 1978, 1982)
Current Status: Retired

Legends of **FOOTBALL**

CARLOS**ALBERTO**

he achieved a certain notoriety with his comments about Michael Owen during the campaign for the 2006 World Cup) during the course of his managerial career. Surprisingly, given the experience he is able to call upon, he has not been requested to take over the biggest coaching role of all, that of the Brazilian side. Whilst the Brazilian FA may not have pencilled in his name for a role, his contemporaries seldom ignore him, with Pelé naming him one of the best 125 living footballers in March 2004 and the US National Soccer Hall of Fame inducting him in 2003.

tournament, if not one of the greatest goals in the history of the competition, with his thunderbolt from the edge of the area against Italy in the 1970 final. It put the seal on a convincing 4-1 victory over the more defence-minded Italians and provided a timely reminder that even at the top level, defenders were not necessarily confined to their own half of the field.

It was a philosophy Carlos took into management himself. He returned to Brazil in 1983 to take over at Flamengo and then managed a number of Brazilian club sides over the next two decades, including Corinthians in 1985 and 1986, Nautico in 1986 and 1987, Botafogo in 1993, 1994, 1997, 1998, 2002 and 2003, Fluminense in 1994 and 1995 and Paysandu in 2005 before returning to Botafogo once again as head coach in 2006. He was also much in demand as a national coach, guiding Nigeria, Oman and Azerbaijan (where of course

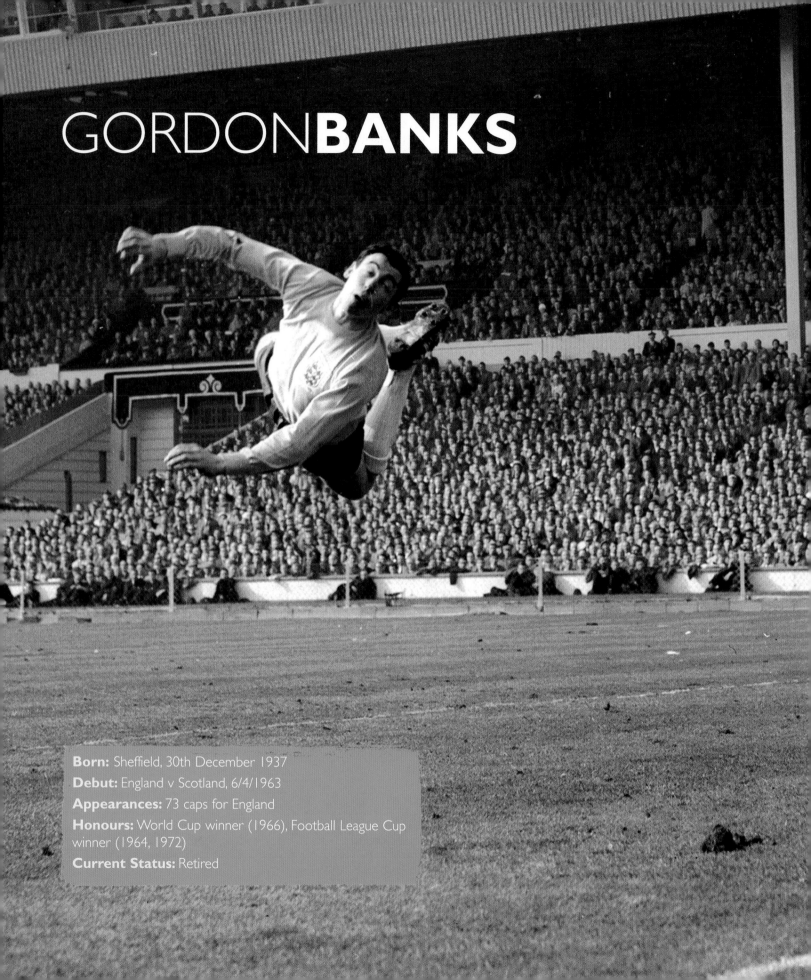

GORDON**BANKS**

Born: Sheffield, 30th December 1937
Debut: England v Scotland, 6/4/1963
Appearances: 73 caps for England
Honours: World Cup winner (1966), Football League Cup winner (1964, 1972)
Current Status: Retired

In a career that lasted some fifteen years and saw him reach the pinnacle of international success, it is Gordon Banks' lot to be remembered for just one save, that against Pelé during the 1970 World Cup finals in Mexico. Those who played in front of him during those fifteen years, for both club and country, never had any doubt that this was the kind of save he pulled off week after week, but the fact that it happened live with the world watching confirmed to a much wider audience that Banks was the best in the world.

Born in Sheffield in 1937 Gordon played schools football in Sheffield before joining Chesterfield in September 1955, helping the club make a surprise run to the FA Youth Cup final the following year, a run that had many other clubs casting an envious eye in his direction. It took just 23 appearances for the Chesterfield first team for Gordon to make an impact on a bigger stage, prompting a £6,000 raid by Leicester City in May 1959, a figure that seems ridiculously low even by the standards in force at the time. Indeed, over the next eight years Gordon not only repaid the transfer fee but added a couple of noughts to his value along the way. In a Leicester side that was little more than average, Gordon was often the difference between victory and defeat, helping the Foxes reach the FA Cup finals of 1961 and 1963 and the League Cup final in 1964 and 1965. Only the 1964 League Cup final was eventually won, proof that whilst Gordon often made miraculous saves he could not always work miracles.

Ron Springett had been England's first choice goalkeeper for some four years before Alf Ramsey decided to ring the changes following a disastrous European Championship qualifying match against France that was lost 5-2 in Paris. Gordon was drafted in for the next match against Scotland in February 1963 and was a virtual ever-present for the next nine years. Indeed, in between his first and last appearances for his country, England played 99 internationals and Gordon was in goal for 73 of them. The phrase 'safe as the Banks of England' was coined in his honour – it was well deserved.

Whilst Gordon was considered a household name in England prior to the World Cup finals of 1966, his steady performances during the competition attracted much admiration on a wider scale. He was seldom troubled in England's first four matches of the competition, against Uruguay, Mexico, France and Argentina, although it has to be said that the entire defence was extremely well marshalled and few attackers got through to fire off a shot. It was in the semi-final that his true worth shone through, for against the

BELOW
Gordon Banks during a training session at Roehampton.

Portuguese he was in superb form, his positional sense, reflexes and agility ensuring the goals against column was kept to the barest minimum. The only time he was beaten was by a penalty, the closest Eusebio got to Gordon all night. His performance in the final against West Germany was equally assured, with Gordon only being beaten by a rasping shot from Helmut Haller after a mistake by Ray Wilson and a late equaliser that appeared to be helped along by a German hand before finding its way into the net.

With England crowned World Champions and Gordon virtually unchallenged as the greatest 'keeper on the planet, Leicester City decided to sell him in April the following year! At the time the transfer to Stoke City for £52,000 created something of a sensation, Leicester claiming that Gordon was almost 30 years of age whilst his club understudy, Peter Shilton, who was ten years his junior, was potentially as good. History shows that Leicester just about got it right with regards to Peter's future, but Gordon too was able to show that goalkeepers don't tail off at the same rate as their outfield counterparts once they get the wrong side of thirty.

Gordon was 32 by the time the 1970 World Cup finals came around, still regarded one of the best in the world and he proved it beyond doubt during the tournament. It was that save from Pelé's header, a dive to the foot of the right hand post to send the ball up

and over the bar, which got the superlatives, especially when it was revealed after the match that Pelé was so sure of his header he was shouting goal as soon as the ball left his head. You couldn't do anything else but just applaud the save, and quite a few Brazilians joined their English counterparts in doing just that. What happened before the quarter-final against West Germany is equally notorious, with many connected with the England side of the time being convinced that Gordon was 'got at' – he was the only player to suffer a mysterious stomach bug when all the players ate the same meals, the belief being that a bottle of beer had been tampered with. Whatever the circumstances, Gordon missed the quarter-final, his replacement had a nightmare and England slipped out of the World Cup.

Gordon was still at the top of his game two years later, helping Stoke City win the only major piece of silverware they've ever collected in their history, the Football League Cup, he was awarded an OBE and was named Footballer of the Year by the Football Writers Association. They weren't to know, but that was something of a swan-song for Gordon, for in October 1972 he was returning home from getting some treatment when his car was involved in an accident, costing Gordon the sight in his right eye. Although he attempted a comeback he was never going to be the same player again and wisely decided to retire in August 1973. Spells in coaching and management followed but he had greater success running a sports promotions company.

ROBERTO**BAGGIO**

Throughout much of the early 1990s, Roberto Baggio, Il Divino Codino (The Divine Ponytail) was virtually unrivalled as one of the best and most technically gifted players in the world, with his skills earning him the adulation of fans wherever he played. His coaches and managers, whilst full of praise for his abilities, often had cause to fall foul of Roberto (and vice versa), but his reputation remained untarnished right through to the end.

Born in Caldogno near Vicenza in 1967, Roberto joined the local club, then playing in Serie C, in 1981. He made just 35 appearances for the club, scoring 13 goals, before the bigger Italian clubs came looking, eventually signing with Fiorentina in 1985.

Whilst Fiorentina were still some way short of a side that could challenge for the top honours on a regular basis, Roberto was on his way to achieving cult status at the club – with Roberto in the side there was always a chance that better things lay around the corner. If domestic success proved somewhat elusive, his contribution did not go unnoticed by his national side, with Roberto being given the first of his 56 caps for his country in 1988.

Robert had scored 39 goals in 94 appearances for Fiorentina when Juventus came knocking on the door in 1990, eventually paying a then world record transfer fee of 15 billion lira ($19 million) to take the player to Turin. The move caused an outcry at Fiorentina, with Roberto reluctantly forced to switch his allegiance; 'I was compelled to accept the transfer' was his comment to the fans he left behind.

At least the switch led to Roberto winning honours at club level (the closest Fiorentina had come during his time with the club was runners-up spot in the UEFA Cup), starting with the UEFA Cup in 1993 after a 6-1 aggregate victory over Borussia Dortmund (3-1 in Dortmund and 3-0 in Turin). This was the culmination of Roberto's greatest season, one which saw him named European Footballer of the Year (the first Italian to have won the honour since Paolo Rossi in 1982) and FIFA World Player of the Year.

By then he was a seasoned Italian international, having helped them finish third in the 1990 competition held in Italy. He netted two goals during the competition, including one reckoned to have been the goal of the competition against Czechoslovakia, and might have finished with a higher tally but for his sportsmanship – although he was the country's designated penalty taker, he stepped aside and allowed Salvatore Schillaci to take one in the third and fourth place play-off against England, which allowed Schillaci to win the Golden Boot award.

By 1994 his was the first name that went onto the team sheet and it was largely his inspiration that propelled Italy into the final. He scored five goals along the way, including the match winner against Spain in

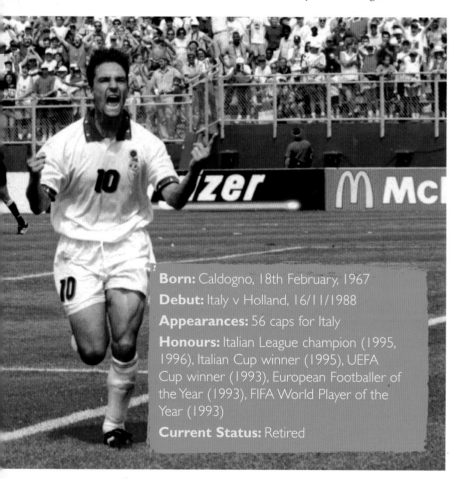

Born: Caldogno, 18th February, 1967
Debut: Italy v Holland, 16/11/1988
Appearances: 56 caps for Italy
Honours: Italian League champion (1995, 1996), Italian Cup winner (1995), UEFA Cup winner (1993), European Footballer of the Year (1993), FIFA World Player of the Year (1993)
Current Status: Retired

upturn in his fortunes and after netting 22 goals during the season, he was included in the Italian World Cup squad for the competition in France, with a starting place in the first match ahead of the young pretender Alessandro Del Piero. He made the first and scored the second in the opening match against Chile, thus becoming the first Italian player to have scored in three World Cup campaigns, but there was heartache further along, with Italy going out of the competition after a penalty shoot out against eventual champions France in the quarter-final. Roberto Baggio's third and final World Cup campaign ended in exactly the same way as his previous two campaigns, beaten in a penalty shoot out, although Roberto did at least score with his effort against France.

Upon returning from international duty Roberto returned to Milan, this time signing for Internazionale, but this was a move that must have been orchestrated by the directors, for coach Marcello Lippi used him sparingly (according to Baggio's autobiography, he was dropped by Lippi for refusing to reveal what his team-mates had said about the coach in private moments). Roberto eventually escaped his Inter hell with a move to Brescia in 2000, but the damage had already been done to his international career. He missed out on selection for the 2002 World Cup finals; although he was 35 by the time the finals kicked off, many felt his experience could have benefited the Italians somewhere along the way.

Roberto Baggio continued at Brescia until 2004, the same year he collected his final cap for his country. By the time he retired, he had hit 205 goals in Serie A for his various clubs (in 318 appearances), making him the fifth highest goalscorer in Italian history.

LEFT
Baggio in action for Italy at the 1994 World Cup.

BELOW
Roberto Baggio salutes the crowd having played his last game for Brescia in 2004.

the quarter-finals and two against Bulgaria in the semi-final. He was patently not fully fit for the final itself against Brazil, but such was his worth to the Italian side he was selected anyway. Unfortunately, in a match that had plenty of action but no goals, it fell to Roberto to miss the vital penalty in the shoot out, striking the bar with his effort and effectively handing Brazil the trophy.

There was compensation of sorts when he helped Juventus win the double of Italian League and Italian Cup in 1995, but before he could turn his attention towards the Champions League, he was on the move again, this time poached by Silvio Berlusconi's AC Milan, having netted 78 goals in his 141 appearances for Juventus. Once again Roberto had been reluctantly moved from one club to another, and although he helped his new club win the League at the end of the season, thus becoming the first player to win consecutive titles with different clubs, his time at AC Milan was not a resounding success.

In 1997, seemingly approaching the twilight of his career he was sold to Bologna. The move resulted in an

GABRIEL**BATISTUTA**

Gabriel Batistuta was an exceptional all-round sportsman as a youngster and at one point considered pursuing a career as a basketball player, but watching his compatriots win the 1978 FIFA World Cup led to a switch to football – his accomplishments since then may have been basketball's loss but they were definitely football's gain.

Born in Avellaneda, a province of Sante Fe, to a slaughterhouse-worker father and school secretary mother, Gabriel moved with his family to Reconquista soon after where he was effectively raised. He also took to playing football in the streets, inspired by the likes of Mario Kempes and his role in winning the 1978 World Cup, and was eventually spotted by junior team Platense. From there he joined the local Reconquista side and helped them win the provincial championship by beating Newell's Old Boys from Rosario in the final and scoring two of the goals.

His performances against Newell's Old Boys prompted a swoop by the Rosario club and Gabriel joined them as a professional in 1988, although he struggled to make an impact with his new club, living away from home, sleeping in the stadium and missing his girlfriend (later his wife), which led to weight problems and a loss of form. Newell's Old Boys sent him on loan to Deportivo Italiano, helping them in the Carnevale Cup in Italy and scoring three goals as he rediscovered his form.

After 24 appearances for Newell's Old Boys (and having scored seven goals) he moved on to River Plate, one of the bigger Argentine clubs and proved an exceptional striker on the field, netting 17 goals in just 21 appearances. He still had problems off the field, often clashing with coach Daniel Passarella, another member of that victorious 1978 side. It was not to be the last clash between Gabriel and Passarella either, with Passarella dropping Gabriel from the River Plate side and eventually letting him move on to bitter rivals Boca Juniors. The Boca Juniors coach Oscar Tabarez gave Gabriel the support he needed and was rewarded with thirteen goals in 34 appearances, culminating in Gabriel breaking into the national side and helping them win the Copa America in 1991.

Among the many interested observers at the 1991 Copa America was the vice-president of Fiorentina, who quickly arranged for Gabriel to move to Italy to join the then Serie A club. Unfortunately the club was relegated into Serie B the following season and did not retain their top flight status until after Claudio Ranieri became coach, with Gabriel netting sixteen of the goals that took them back.

By the time of the 1994 World Cup Gabriel was a regular in the Argentine side, having helped them win

Born: Avellaneda, Santa Fe, 1st February 1969
Debut: Argentina v Brazil, 27/6/1991
Appearances: 78 caps for Argentina
Honours: Italian League champion (2001), Italian Super Cup winner (2001), Italian Cup winner (1996), Argentine Footballer of the Year (1998), Copa America winner (1991, 1993)
Current Status: Retired

Legends of **FOOTBALL**

When Gabriel was in the side he responded the best way he knew how, scoring five goals during the 1998 competition, including a hat-trick against Jamaica, as Argentina made the quarter-final.

Back in Italy Fiorentina's failure to mount a serious challenge for the League title prompted Gabriel to look for a bigger club to join, but the appointment of Giovanni Trapattoni seemed to herald a concerted effort to lift the title. Fiorentina were there or thereabouts for long spells of the 1999-2000 season, but an injury to Gabriel kept him out for a month and Fiorentina slipped to third in his absence. At the end of the season he departed the club, moving on to AS Roma for $35 million, having scored 168 goals in his 269 appearances.

Gabriel did finally get to win the Italian League at the end of his season with the club, their first such success since 1983, with Gabriel netting twenty of the goals that made it possible. The following year it was international matters that concentrated his mind, trying to help Argentina in the 2002 World Cup. He scored a number of vital goals that earned qualification under coach Marcelo Bielsa, but the team were eliminated from the so-called group of death against England, Sweden and Nigeria, their first first-round exit since 1962. That brought the end of his international career, with just two Copa Americas having been won despite his 56 goals in 78 appearances.

Whether he was suffering a fall out from his international exploits will never be known but he struggled for form back in Italy, being sent on loan to Inter before heading off to Qatar where injuries eventually brought an end to his playing career in 2005. He later moved to Australia and was rumoured to be trying to buy the Perth Glory franchise club.

LEFT
Gabriel Batistuta celebrating with his team mates after Argentina won the COPA America final in 1993.

BELOW
Batistuta in action for Qatar's al-Arabi club.

two Copa Americas, but Argentina's quest for the World Cup came to an embarrassing end following Diego Maradona's positive dope test. Despite this disappointment at international level Gabriel returned to Italy in the best form of his career, finishing top goalscorer in 1995 and helping Fiorentina win the Italian Cup and Super Cup in 1996.

There were to be further disappointments on the international scene, with the appointment of Daniel Passarella seeing Gabriel dropped almost as regularly as he played, with Passarella refusing to pick players who had long hair or wore earrings among his 'house rules'.

FRANZ**BECKENBAUER**

Born: Munich, 11th September 1945

Debut: Sweden v West Germany 26/9/1965

Appearances: 103 for West Germany

Honours: World Cup winner (1974), European Championship winner (1972), European Cup winner (1974, 1975, 1976), European Cup Winners' Cup winner (1967), League Champion (1969, 1972, 1973, 1974), Soccer Bowl winner (1977, 1978, 1980)

Current Status: Retired

A cultured, elegant and dominant player, Franz Beckenbauer was given the nickname 'Der Kaiser' (the Emperor), a name that perfectly described his playing style. Born in Munich he began his career with SC Munich '06 before being snapped up by Bayern Munich's youth side at the age of fourteen. After appearances in the Regional Liga Süd he was drafted into the first team in the Bundesliga in 1965 and made such an impact that he was capped by the full West German side before the year was out.

Franz's timing was impeccable, for it meant he became a key member of the side that would compete in the 1966 World Cup finals in England. Then he was something of an attacking midfield player, creating chances for the likes of Uwe Seeler and Helmut Haller but also expected to weigh in with goals of his own. That he did all the way through to the final, but instead of playing to Franz's strengths, he was assigned a man marking job on Bobby Charlton. Whilst he managed to keep Charlton quiet pretty much throughout the whole of the match, his own attacking instincts were blunted and the Germans eventually lost 4-2. It was a mistake they almost made all over again four years later.

After disappointment at international level Franz returned to Munich and set about turning Bayern Munich into the major force in West German football and one of the top sides in Europe. The Bundesliga was first won in 1969 and there was a hat-trick of successes, from 1972 to 1974, before the team achieved the pinnacle of club football, a hat-trick of successes in the European Cup in 1974 through to 1976. They had

already tasted European success before that, having lifted the European Cup Winners' Cup in 1967 after beating Liverpool in the final.

West Germany were one of the original favourites to win the 1970 World cup in Mexico. In the quarter-final against England Franz was again given the task of shadowing an ageing Bobby Charlton around the field, a task that finally ended when Charlton was substituted by Alf Ramsey, supposedly to rest him in time for the semi-final (England were 2-1 ahead). However, freed from his defensive shackles, Franz ventured further and further upfield and was instrumental in getting the Germans back from the dead, finally winning 3-2 in extra time. Unfortunately Franz did not enjoy such freedom in the semi-final against Italy, dislocating a shoulder and being off the field for a time before bravely returning to the fray. Sadly, West Germany lost 4-3 in one of the great World Cup matches and had to contend themselves with finishing third after a 1-0 win over Uruguay.

BELOW
Franz Beckenbauer and the West German team with the World Cup trophy in Munich, West Germany, 1974.

Four years later, in their own backyard, the West Germans beat Holland 2-1 after going a goal down in a downpour to enable Franz as captain (he took over the role in 1971) to get his hands on the World Cup Trophy. It was not the first trophy Franz had collected as captain either, for two years previously he had helped the Germans to success in the European Championship, beating the Russians 3-0 in the final.

The West German side peaked with that 1974 World Cup win, for the 1976 European Championship final was lost and a year later Franz was on his way to America to join the North American Soccer League with New York Cosmos. He may have won the US Soccer Bowl three times in his four seasons, but it hardly compared with his former glories. He returned home to join Hamburger SV in 1980, retiring from playing in 1983 having made 103 appearances for his country and 424 appearances for his clubs.

He then became manager of the national side, guiding them to the final of the World Cup in 1986 in Mexico where they lost to Argentina. Four years later, in Italy, they exacted the perfect revenge in beating the same opponents in a miserable final by one goal to nil, the only goal coming from a hotly disputed penalty. The circumstances of the win would not have mattered to Franz Beckenbauer – he became one of only two men to have won the World Cup as a player and a coach.

Franz wisely left the national job at that point and went into club management with Olympique Marseille

LEFT
Beckenbauer fights
for the ball with
Moroccan Benkhrif
Boujemaa, 1970.

FAR LEFT
Beckenbauer runs
onto the pitch for
the New York
Cosmos, 1978.

BELOW
Bayern Munich captain
Franz Beckenbauer
holds the European
Cup aloft in 1975.

in 1990 but left a year later. There was no surprise when
he returned to Bayern Munich in 1992, subsequently
becoming club president in 1994. Later appointments
included becoming Vice President of the DFB and head
of the German bid team that successfully won the right
to stage the 2006 World Cup finals. He will serve as
chairman of the organising committee during the
competition. Voted the second best European player of
the last fifty years in a 2004 poll, there are rumours that
Franz Beckenbauer has one further job vacancy to fill
before he finally retires; President of UEFA when
Lennart Johansson himself retires in 2006.

Legends of **FOOTBALL**

DAVID
BECKHAM

Born: Leytonstone, London, 2nd May 1975

Debut: Moldova v England, 1/9/1996

Appearances: 94 caps for England

Honours: European Champions League winner (1999), Premier League Champion (1996, 1997, 1999, 2000, 2001, 2003), FA Cup winner (1996, 1999)

Current Status: Still playing

Probably the most instantly recognisable player on the planet, David trained with Spurs as a youngster but set his heart on signing for Manchester United, duly being taken on a trainee in January 1993 having already helped the club win the FA Youth Cup in 1992. He was loaned out to Preston North End in February 1995 but returned to Old Trafford and broke into the first team on a regular basis by the end of the season.

The following season David was one of the midfield stars as United won the Premier League and FA Cup double, with his performances at club level earning him his first full cap for England in September 1996. The Premier League was retained at the end of the season and David's profile, already huge because of playing for Manchester United, went into overdrive with his relationship with the then Spice Girl singer and later wife Victoria Adams. His good looks also made him a target for a slew of sponsors, and not necessarily from the sporting world as ties with the likes of Brylcream would confirm.

By now a regular in the England side, David had mixed fortunes during the 1998 World Cup, being omitted from the opening match after his manager claimed he wasn't 'focused enough' but scored a stunning free kick in England's third group match to ensure their progress into the knockout stage. There he allowed himself to react to an Argentine tackle from Diego Simeone and was sent off at a crucial point in the game. Whether or not England would have gone on to win with him still on the field is a matter of debate, but certain sections of the media and public held him

accountable and for a number of months he had to live with effigies being hung in certain streets and death threats received by his club.

His popularity at Manchester United was not affected by the events in France and in 1999 he helped the club win the treble of Premier League, FA Cup and European Champions League. United repeated their League successes in 2000 and 2001, by which time David was well on his way to reclaiming his popularity mantle, finally achieved with a last gasp free kick against Greece that ensured England's place in the 2002 World Cup finals. England were drawn in the same group as Argentina and provided David with the perfect opportunity to exorcise that particular ghost when a superbly struck penalty gave England a 1-0 victory.

Just as his star rose again on the international front, so there was a dimming of his relationship with his club manager Sir Alex Ferguson. This boiled over in one post-match inquest, with Sir Alex accidentally kicking a football boot that hit David square in the face and

DAVID**BECKHAM**

required a number of butterfly stitches. Although Manchester United won their domestic Championship at the end of the season, Sir Alex had expressed himself dissatisfied with the so-called media circus that accompanied David and his wife Victoria with almost as many column inches being devoted to the couple's children. Although there were believed to be many clubs lining up with offers, United finally settled on one of £25 million from Real Madrid in the summer of 2003.

Whilst the media circus still rolls in and out of town, there have been considerable benefits to Real Madrid since they signed David Beckham. The trophy room may be bare, with Real Madrid currently languishing behind their bitter rivals Barcelona, but the bank balance is more than healthy with the club having taken a reported £100 million in replica shirt sales since David arrived at the club. Indeed, such has been David's impact off the field, Real Madrid have overtaken Manchester United as the most popular club side in the world, even if achievements on it still leave a lot to be desired.

David's worth to the England national side is not to be under estimated. The general consensus is that his best position is on the right hand side of midfield, where his ability to deliver the ball with pace and swerve is a vital part of the national armoury. David however favours a more central position, although the two occasions it was tried resulted in a lopsided England performance, with David, Steven Gerrard and Frank Lampard getting in each other's way and England struggling to a 1-0 victory over Wales and suffering a similar scoreline defeat to Northern Ireland.

In October 2005 he achieved the unwelcome distinction of becoming the first England player to be sent off twice, but where there was vilification after his first dismissal, his second brought only sympathy, for he was felt to have been harshly booked in the two incidents that led to the obligatory red card. England held on to win the match and group and qualify for the 2006 World Cup finals.

In what was the last tournament for head coach Sven Goran Eriksson, his hopes of going out on the ultimate high, with the World Cup duly delivered for the first time in forty years, depended largely on the abilities of David Beckham.

David experienced mixed fortunes during the tournament, scoring against Paraguay but suffering an injury that brought an end to his dreams in the next round. In January 2007 it was announced that he was leaving Real Madrid for American side Los Angeles Galaxy in a deal worth a reported $250 million.

GEORGE**BEST**

Born: Belfast, 22nd May 1946

Died: 25th November 2005

Debut: Wales v Northern Ireland, 15/4/1964

Appearances: 37 caps for Northern Ireland

Honours: Football League Champion (1965, 1967),
European Cup winner (1968), Football Writers'
Association Player of the Year 1968, European Footballer
of the Year 1968

Current Status: Deceased

The most charismatic player ever to grace a football field, George Best was the player who had it all and seemingly threw it all away. That is if the media are to be believed, for whilst George hit the headlines for all the wrong reasons after he hung up his boots, there was hardly a moment in his life that he regretted.

Discovered by Manchester United scout Bob Bishop in Belfast at the age of fifteen, George's abilities were such that Bishop sent United manager Matt Busby a telegram that simple read 'I have found a genius.' It was to prove something of an understatement, but George's career could well have been over before it had even begun, with the homesick young Irishman running back to Belfast within a couple of weeks of his arrival in Manchester. Matt Busby persevered, allowing the then shy footballer time off to visit home and recharge his batteries. It was to prove a masterstroke, for by the time George had conquered his homesickness he had filled out into a physique that was the epitome of the perfect footballer; gifted with either foot, difficult to knock off the ball and possessing a wonderful sense of balance.

He made his debut for United in 1963 against West Bromwich Albion and would go on to make 466 appearances for the club, scoring a remarkable 178 goals. What made his goalscoring abilities all the more impressive was the fact that he was not an out and out goalscorer but was in the team for his abilities to create chances for others, but George was often the quickest to move into space he had created and finish off the chance himself. Top goalscorer for his club in six successive seasons, he topped the First Division charts in 1967-68 with 28 goals. That,

of course, was the season that culminated with victory in the European Cup against Benfica, with George scoring a trademark goal that took him around defenders and the goalkeeper with ease before slotting into an open net. Benfica feared George Best more than any other player in the United side and with good reason; three years earlier George had single-handedly dismantled Benfica in front of their own fans, inspiring United to a 5-1 victory in a European Cup match that Matt Busby had asked his United side to play cautiously to quieten the home side fans!

Dubbed El Beatle by the Portuguese media after the match, that game probably encapsulated everything George Best was about; ignore the pre-match team talk and just go out and take the other side apart. Matt Busby learned to live with his maverick star, even if defences the world over couldn't. Busby got his rewards in the shape of two League titles and the European Cup, but after Busby retired so the cracks in George's make-up came to the surface. Success brought adulation and

BELOW
George Best about to score his third goal (of six) for Manchester United during their Fifth Round FA Cup match against Fourth Division Northampton Town. The final score was 8-2.

adulation brought a whole new set of problems for George to contend with. Interests outside football began to occupy him, including opening a boutique and a nightclub and time was spent at both ventures that should have been spent on the training field. George began skipping training and, in his own words, 'I used to go missing a lot…Miss Canada, Miss United Kingdom, Miss World…'

In 1974 matters came to a head with George being sacked by Manchester United because of his misdemeanours, although initially they believed he might be coaxed back into the game and held on to his registration for a short while. When it became obvious George would not be returning to Old Trafford, his registration was cancelled.

That eventually prompted George to attempt a comeback, but the quality of sides he ended up playing for were not in United's class – there was non-League Dunstable Town, Stockport County, the Los Angeles Aztecs, Fort Lauderdale Strikers and San Jose Earthquakes. He might have scored one of the goals of his career whilst playing in America, beating virtually the entire opposition side during one of his runs, but it could never compare with scoring in the European Cup final.

About the only club with which George enhanced his reputation was Fulham, whom George joined in September 1976 and played 42 matches alongside the equally wayward Rodney Marsh. It was a time of winning friends more than winning points, with Fulham a must see opposition for the Second Division during George and Rodney's time with the club.

George eventually wound up his League career with Bournemouth and officially retired in 1983. He did so having never graced the world stage at international

LEFT
George Best
playing for Manchester
United in 1968
against Everton at
Old Trafford.

FAR LEFT
George Best in action
for the Fort Lauderdale
Strikers in Fort
Lauderdale, Florida,
USA, 1975.

BELOW
Best of Manchester
United pictured
in 1964.

level, although there were calls for George to try and get himself fit enough to be considered for selection for the 1982 World Cup squad in Spain. George ignored those calls, reasoning that the players who had got Northern Ireland to the finals deserved their time in the spotlight, rather than relying on a player who was 36 years of age and past his best.

Life after football saw George make just as many headlines as he had during his prime, but invariably these were for all the wrong reasons. There was a brief spell in prison for assaulting a police officer, his well publicised marriages and relationships that invariably ended in tears and his ongoing battle with alcoholism. Given that he had a liver transplant and continued to drink at the same level as before, it was a one way battle and George ultimately died on 25th November 2005 (ironically the day before all-day drinking was legalised!). A crowd of more than 100,000 turned out to line the streets of Belfast for his funeral, preferring to remember George Best for the irreverent football star he had been, not the man he became.

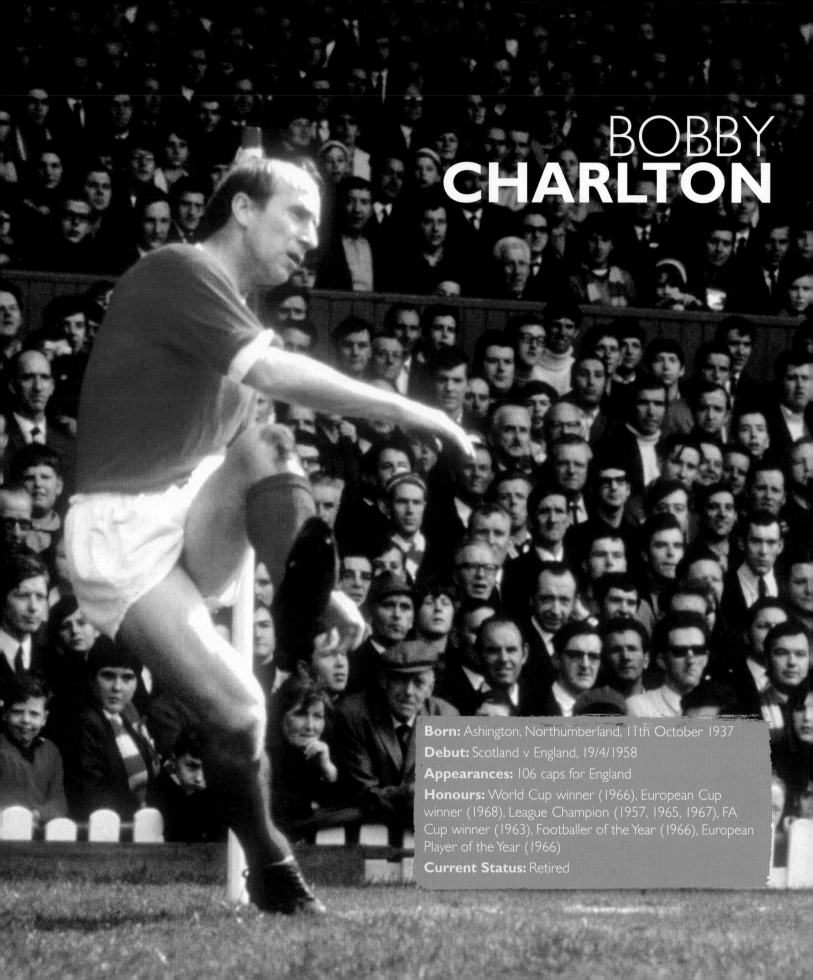

BOBBY
CHARLTON

Born: Ashington, Northumberland, 11th October 1937

Debut: Scotland v England, 19/4/1958

Appearances: 106 caps for England

Honours: World Cup winner (1966), European Cup winner (1968), League Champion (1957, 1965, 1967), FA Cup winner (1963), Footballer of the Year (1966), European Player of the Year (1966)

Current Status: Retired

By way of contrast to George Best, his Manchester United team-mate, Bobby Charlton was the model professional and never gave any of his managers a moments trouble or worry. To many people he is Manchester United and continues to serve the club more than fifty years since he first arrived.

A nephew of the famous Jackie Milburn, Bobby was something of a child prodigy and represented England at schoolboy and youth level before he signed professional forms with Manchester United. He joined the club straight from school and helped them win the FA Youth Cup in three consecutive years, 1954 to 1956, a time when United were the dominant youth side, winning the trophy in its first five seasons.

It was thus as one of the famed Busby Babes that Bobby made his League debut in October 1956 against Charlton Athletic and scored twice in the 4-2 win. Despite this promising start, Busby was reluctant to over-expose the young striker and Bobby had to contend with irregular starts in the first team. He became a more permanent fixture towards the end of the season as United retained their First Division League title and headed towards a possible League and Cup double. Bobby only owed his place in the final line-up owing to an injury to Dennis Viollet but he made the most of his appearance at Wembley, even if he could do little to prevent United going down to a surprise 2-1 defeat to Aston Villa.

Then 1957-58 was to have been a triumphant march towards success on a number of fronts for United, with progress being made in the European Cup and handily placed in the League race by the time the New Year came.

All those dreams were to end in Munich, where United's plane crashed on take-off whilst the team were returning from their match against Red Star Belgrade. Bobby was thrown fifty yards out of the plane and suffered no more than a deep cut to his head, but eight of his team-mates, including six who had lined up alongside him in the FA Cup final the previous season, ultimately lost their lives.

Although no doubt traumatised by the experience, Bobby picked up the pieces of his career almost immediately, collecting his first full cap for England barely two months after the disaster. Bobby was also able to help propel a makeshift United side to Wembley for the FA Cup final but despite the entire country willing them to victory, Bolton won 2-0.

It was to take Matt Busby five years to assemble another side good enough to win honours, effectively rebuilding the side around those who survived Munich, with Bobby Charlton very much a part of the team. There was at last an FA Cup final victory to savour in 1963 against Leicester City, a match United had

BELOW
Bobby Charlton playing for England in 1964.

actually gone into as underdogs having only just staved off relegation! That FA Cup victory became the springboard for further success, with United winning the League title in 1965 for the first time in eight years.

League success brought another tilt at the European Cup the following season, but once again United were to fall at the semi-final stage. More than adequate compensation was received, at least on a personal note, that same summer as Bobby was an integral part of the England side that was hosting the World Cup finals.

Indeed, Bobby fulfilled much the same role for Alf Ramsey and England as he did for Busby and United. Not quite an out and out striker by now, he could still be relied upon to pop up here and there with vital goals, and nowhere was this more evident than during the World Cup. Scorer of England's first goal in the competition against Mexico, Bobby struck two in the semi-final against Portugal, a match that was probably Bobby's best in an England shirt. His second goal, a thunderbolt shot taken on the run was so good even several of the Portuguese side shook his hand as he made his way back to the halfway line!

His performance in the semi-final resulted in the West German side detailing the young midfield player Franz Beckenbauer to keep Bobby in check. Bobby had a quiet match, so in one sense Franz had done his job, but equally, by concentrating on what Bobby Charlton was doing Franz Beckenbauer was unable to assist his own team up front as he had done previously in the competition – Bobby Charlton probably made a greater contribution to England's eventual success than even he realised.

United won the League title again in 1967 and went into the European Cup the following season, the tenth anniversary of the Munich disaster, looking for a

tangible way to mark the occasion. This time around the semi-final stage was breached, United overcoming the odds and Real Madrid at the Bernabeu Stadium to make the final, against Benfica at Wembley. Although the match went to extra time, Bobby Charlton, Matt Busby and Manchester United were not to be denied their destiny, Bobby scoring twice in the 4-1 victory. As captain he got to lift the trophy, but the sight of the evening was the hug between Busby and his captain; they had survived Munich together and finally exorcised the memory of that fateful day.

If Bobby Charlton had retired there and then his story would have been perfect. He played on until 1973, but United were never to hit those heights again and Bobby's final five years were devoid of trophies. His international career carried on until 1970, in the World Cup against West Germany, but this time Alf Ramsey took off Bobby when England were 2-1 ahead to supposedly save his legs for the expected semi-final. Freed of marking duties on Bobby Charlton, Franz Beckenbauer began dictating the match and inspired the Germans to a 3-2 victory.

By the time Bobby left Old Trafford he had made a record 606 League appearances for United and a then record 106 appearances for England, hitting 199 goals for club and 49 for country, both of which are still records. He went on to become player-manager of Preston North End but found he wasn't cut out for the role, duly retiring in 1975. Knighted in 1994 (he had previously been made a CBE) Bobby spent spells on the board at Wigan Athletic before ultimately finding his way back to his beloved Old Trafford, fulfilling a role today that fellow knight Matt Busby had held a decade earlier.

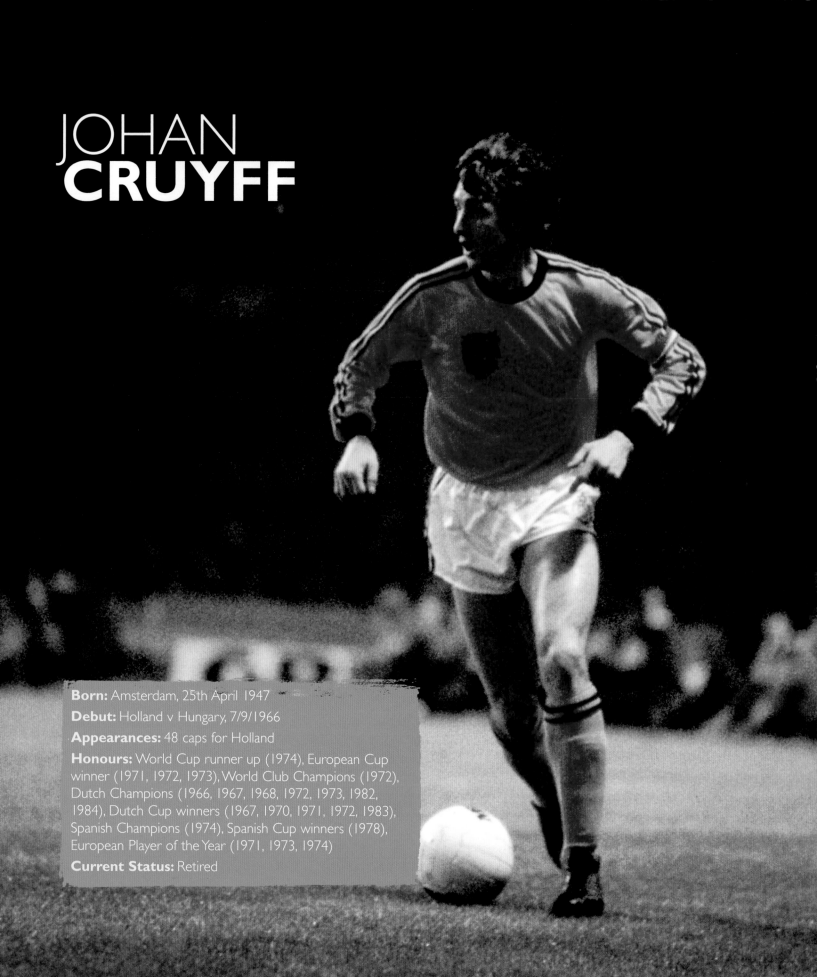

JOHAN
CRUYFF

Born: Amsterdam, 25th April 1947

Debut: Holland v Hungary, 7/9/1966

Appearances: 48 caps for Holland

Honours: World Cup runner up (1974), European Cup winner (1971, 1972, 1973), World Club Champions (1972), Dutch Champions (1966, 1967, 1968, 1972, 1973, 1982, 1984), Dutch Cup winners (1967, 1970, 1971, 1972, 1983), Spanish Champions (1974), Spanish Cup winners (1978), European Player of the Year (1971, 1973, 1974)

Current Status: Retired

If Pelé was the world's greatest player of the 1960s, then Johan Cruyff was his natural successor the following decade, inspiring his **Ajax** club side to three consecutive European Cups and his **Dutch** national side to the final of the **World Cup**. Unlike Pelé, however, **Cruyff** just fell short of collecting the ultimate prize in football.

Born close to Ajax's ground in Amsterdam, his mother was a cleaner at the club and persuaded Ajax to take Johan into their youth coaching scheme at the age of 12. It was English coach Vic Buckingham that further persuaded the club to take him on as a professional and by the age of 17 Johan had made his debut for the first team. Two years later came the first of his 48 caps for his country and Johan marked the occasion by scoring a last minute equaliser in the 2-2 draw.

It is of course with Ajax that he initially made his reputation, a club side that first introduced the football world to the concept of 'Total Football.' Guided by coach Rinus Michels, Ajax developed a side where all the players were of the same technical ability and therefore able to play in any position with equal effectiveness. Cruyff's role in the side was officially centre forward, but since he often popped up wide on either flank, the man assigned to mark him didn't know whether to follow Cruyff out to the wing or sit where he was and pick up whoever appeared in the hole. Defences across Europe were similarly caught in two minds and Ajax exploited the confusion to the full. Runners-up in the 1969 European Cup final against AC Milan, the following four years saw Dutch domination of the premier club

competition in Europe, with Ajax' fiercest rivals Feyenoord beating Celtic 2-1 in 1970 and Ajax overcoming Panathinakos, Inter Milan and Juventus 2-0, 2-0 and 1-0 respectively in lifting the trophy three years in succession. Cruyff made his impact felt especially in the clashes with the Italians, being credited with taking Inter apart almost single-handedly as well as scoring both goals in 1972 and inspiring one of the greatest twenty-minute spells of football ever seen in the 1-0 win over Juventus. Not for nothing did he become known as Pythagorus in Boots.

After the 1973 victory Johan followed manager Rinus Michels to Barcelona, costing the Catalan club a then record fee of £922,300, also being joined by fellow Ajax play Johan Neeskens. The Spanish season had already started by the time Cruyff arrived and the club were well down the table, but Cruyff inspired a great turn-around and by the end of the season Barcelona were Champions, a 5-0 victory over Real Madrid being the undoubted highlight of the campaign.

BELOW

Cruyff in action for Ajax during the 1970s.

The summer of 1974 saw the World Cup being played in West Germany. Holland had one of the best sides in the world, as they would prove, but they were not the best of teams, with the Ajax and Feyenoord players refusing to mix with one another and the whole squad being unsettled by bonus negotiations that dragged on and on. Holland also had something of a struggle in qualifying, being held home and away by Belgium, but eventually qualified for the finals for the first time since 1938.

Their performance in the first group phase saw them post notice that they were there for the long haul, beating an aggressive Uruguayan side 2-0 and the luckless Bulgarians 4-0, the 0-0 draw with Sweden doing nothing to impede their progress into the second phase. They were even more impressive in that round, thumping Argentina 4-0, the East Germans 2-0 and then eliminated the holders Brazil 2-0. This was not the samba swaying Brazil the world had fallen in love with of four years previously but a hacking and kicking Brazilian side that ultimately got what

they deserved, Neeskens and Cruyff scoring the goals that took Holland into the final.

There they met the host nation in a match that was effectively billed as a personal battle between Franz Beckenbauer and Johan Cruyff. Cruyff had the first word, setting in motion a move from the kick off that saw fifteen completed passes by the Dutch before Cruyff was scythed down by Hoeness for a penalty that Neeskens duly despatched. For twenty minutes or so Holland kept up the torment but without adding to their score, allowing the Germans to grow in confidence and get back into the game. An equalising penalty was followed by a winner from Gerd Muller and it was Beckenbauer, not Cruyff, who got to lift the new World Cup trophy at the end of the match.

Johan Cruyff did not appear in the next tournament in Argentina, withdrawing from the squad in protest at the military coup that had taken place in the host nation, but his Dutch countrymen still played the same kind of total football that again carried them into the final. There they were beaten in extra time by Argentina, but it is worth considering how much better the Dutch might have done had Cruyff been on the pitch.

Johan initially retired from football in 1978 in order to concentrate on his business interests but changed his mind a year later and went to play in the North American leagues. After a brief spell in Spain Johan returned to Ajax in 1981, then aged 34, but still had enough guile to lead the club to League and club success. He could even switch to bitter rivals Feyenoord

and take them to the League title, alongside a player who would eventually become his logical successor, Ruud Gullit.

When he finally finished playing Johan turned to coaching and became a success all over again, taking Ajax to the European Cup Winners' Cup in 1987 and, most notably, Barcelona to the one trophy they desired above all others, the European Cup in 1992 – four Spanish titles and the European Cup Winners' Cup counting for little in the minds of those who followed the club.

With hindsight Johan should have perhaps quit the Barcelona job on the night he delivered the European Cup. Rumours abounded that he was going to coach the Dutch national side in the 1994 World Cup finals but

was unable to agree terms. Two years later, with Barcelona out of the League title race for the second year in succession, he was sacked, a less than glorious end for the man who had given them so much.

The abiding memory of Johan Cruyff, however, is not the chain smoking manager and coach on the sidelines imploring his side on. It is the centre forward who appears out on the left wing and makes as though he is going to cross the ball right footed into the centre but, all in one motion, drags the ball through his own legs, turns 180 degrees and tears off down the wing leaving a bemused defender sitting on the grass wondering where the man he was marking has gone. That is why Johan Cruyff deserved all of the accolades that came his way during the 1970s.

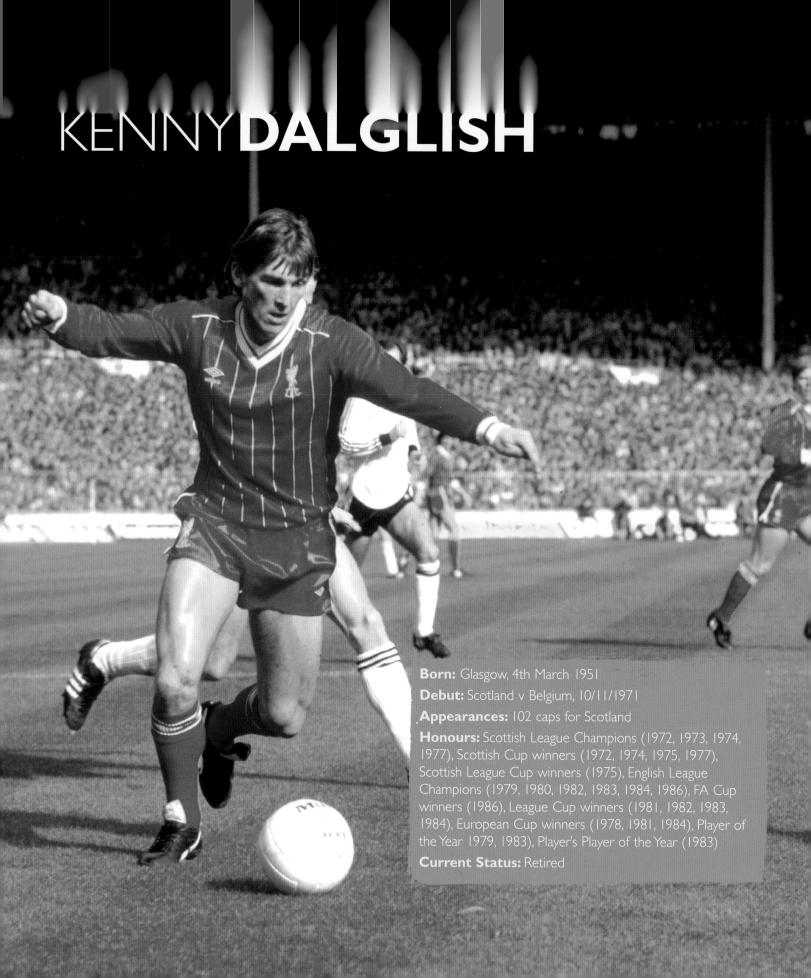

KENNY**DALGLISH**

Born: Glasgow, 4th March 1951

Debut: Scotland v Belgium, 10/11/1971

Appearances: 102 caps for Scotland

Honours: Scottish League Champions (1972, 1973, 1974, 1977), Scottish Cup winners (1972, 1974, 1975, 1977), Scottish League Cup winners (1975), English League Champions (1979, 1980, 1982, 1983, 1984, 1986), FA Cup winners (1986), League Cup winners (1981, 1982, 1983, 1984), European Cup winners (1978, 1981, 1984), Player of the Year 1979, 1983), Player's Player of the Year (1983)

Current Status: Retired

It is arguable whether Liverpool ever had a better player in their entire history, for when Kenny Dalglish arrived in 1977 for a then British record fee of £440,000, he was already the finished article and slotted into the Liverpool side as though born for the role. Then it was revealed Liverpool could have had him for nothing some eleven years previously – he had been born for the role!

Born in Glasgow Kenny was a fan of Rangers as a youngster, not surprising as he was brought up not far from Ibrox. He excelled as a youngster, albeit as a goalkeeper, but had switched to outfield, as a right half, by the time he won his first schoolboy cap at the age of 15. Not long after he was invited down to Liverpool for a trial, making a single appearance for the B team in a match against Southport Reserves, but even though Bill Shankly watched him he was allowed to return home. He also failed a trial with West Ham and sat at home hoping that Rangers might make a move.

In the end it was their bitterest rivals Celtic who knocked on the door, with assistant manager Sean Fallon sent by Jock Stein to sign the youngster up. It was not all plain sailing, for Kenny was reluctant to let the Celtic man inside the house (which, according to legend, was bedecked with pictures of Rangers' heroes!) and it took three hours before he finally put pen to paper – Fallon's wife and children had sat outside the house in the car for the whole time and were not best pleased either!

Kenny was sent out to Cumbernauld United, a Celtic nursery side and also worked as an apprentice joiner whilst working at his preferred profession of football. It was to take him three years to break into the first team, but once in, he was there for good. In 1972 he helped the club win the domestic double, repeating the feat in 1974 and 1977, the latter year as captain, having been made skipper at the start of the 1975-76 season. Already, however, Kenny was beginning to get restless, for he had signed for Celtic just after their European Cup success and wanted some of the same for himself – he believed Celtic were unlikely to be able to recapture that particular trophy.

According to another legend, not long after he had made his Celtic breakthrough Liverpool manager Bill Shankly had demanded to know of his scouts why Dalglish hadn't been spotted – when it was pointed out that Kenny had been for a trial at Anfield and that Shankly himself had passed on him, Shankly went into a rage, blaming everyone else at the club for missing out on such a talent. Liverpool did keep tabs on Kenny Dalglish however, and when they learned he could be

BELOW
Kenny Dalglish playing for Liverpool in 1980.

persuaded to leave, stepped in with their £440,000 offer in the summer of 1977. By then Bob Paisley had taken over as manager and Kenny was bought to replace the German-bound Kevin Keegan.

Kenny Dalglish made an instant impact, scoring seven minutes into his debut away at Middlesbrough and also scoring on his home debut, silencing those who doubted his ability to replace King Kevin. By the end of the season it was King Kenny as Liverpool retained the European Cup, even though they missed out on winning the League Cup, beaten by Nottingham Forest after a replay. That was the start of a purple patch for Liverpool, for over the next eight years they were to win the League title six times, the League Cup four times, the European Cup a further two times and the FA Cup once for good measure.

Bob Paisley had handed over the reins to Joe Fagan in 1983 and he had delivered a unique treble of League, League Cup and European Cup at the end of his first season in charge. Liverpool made it to the final of the European Cup in 1985 too, but in the wake of the Heysel Stadium disaster, Fagan stepped down. In his place came Kenny Dalglish, appointed player-manager. At the end of his first season in charge, he took

dedicate the victory to those who lost their lives in Sheffield, it was no consolation. Kenny took Liverpool to the League title for the 18th time in their history the following season, but already the signs were there that he no longer cared for the stress of being manager. In February 1991, whilst still in pursuit of a second double, he sensationally quit the club. Eight months later he sensationally returned to football, but lower down the scale, as manager of Second Division Blackburn Rovers. He took them up into the top flight in 1992 and three years later won the Premier League, being crowned Champions at Anfield despite losing on the day.

Kenny then moved sideways at the club, becoming Director of Football and allowing his assistant Ray Harford to take over as manager. With little or nothing to do, Kenny eventually left the club, only to be lured back into management with Newcastle United in 1997, replacing Kevin Keegan, just as he had done some twenty years previously. Whilst the attraction of becoming the first man to guide three different sides to the League title obviously appealed, Kenny didn't get the chance to fulfil the dream, spending a little over a year at the club before walking away. Apart from a brief spell in charge at Celtic, where he was also on the board, that signalled the end of his involvement in the game.

If his club career was a never ending story of success, the same could not be said for his international career. Whilst Kenny was the first player to win as many as 100 caps, finishing with 102, and was also top scorer for his country with 30 goals, Scotland never managed to make it beyond the second stage of any major tournament, although Kenny did manage to play in the World Cup campaigns of 1974, 1978 and 1982. He could have gone to Mexico in 1986 but was omitted from the squad by temporary manager Alex Ferguson, even though he made appearances for the national side the following season.

It is therefore for his club exploits that Kenny Dalglish will forever be remembered – ten League titles and three European Cups as a player earned him three Player of the Year accolades, whilst two additional League titles earned him Manager of the Year awards. They never knew what they missed at Rangers.

Liverpool to the domestic double, scoring the goal that clinched the League at Chelsea.

Three years later Kenny had his own off field turmoil to contend with, leading both the club and the city in the aftermath of the Hillsborough disaster. Although Liverpool eventually went on to win the FA Cup and

DIDI

Whilst Pelé and Garrincha may have been the samba stars of Brazil's World Cup triumph of 1958, success could not have been achieved without an array of experienced professionals around them, and no one typified this more than Valdir Pereira, the player they called Didi.

Born in Rio de Janeiro in 1929 Didi was very nearly lost to the game at an early age, for he took a bad kick to the knee at just fourteen during an amateur game and an abscess developed. For a time it looked as though he might have to have his right leg amputated but slowly he recovered, spending six months in a wheelchair whilst he was nursed back to full health.

After being pronounced fit Didi set about pursuing a career as a professional and at 18 signed with the local club Americano of Campos. He later moved on to

Lencoense and then Madureira in 1949, subsequently joining the top flight club Fluminense in 1950. It was here that he worked on his particular speciality, the folha seca (falling leaf) free kick, which would curve and then fade, spending hours working on his own to perfect the kick.

Although Didi was too young to play for the Brazil side in the 1950 World Cup finals being staged in the country, he did make his mark on the tournament, being selected for a side of young professionals who played the first match at the famous Maracana Stadium and scoring the first goal.

Didi made his full debut for Brazil two years later against Mexico in the Pan-American championships and became a virtual regular thereafter. He was thus a member of the World Cup side that journeyed to Switzerland for the 1954 competition and was acknowledged as one of Brazil's better performers, although they were eliminated in the quarter-finals in a bruising clash with Hungary.

Two years later Didi was transferred to Botafogo where he helped them win the Carioca championship in 1957 (he had been a member of the Fluminense side that won it in 1951) and then scored one of the most vital goals of his career, the winner in a World Cup qualifying match against Peru that earned Brazil its place in the finals in Sweden in 1958.

The history books show Brazil won the competition, with Pelé netting two goals in the final against the host nation, but it was Didi who made the victory possible, providing the crucial link between attack and defence and lifting his side after they had fallen a goal behind very early on in the final. Didi had collected the ball from the back of the net and as he made his way back to the halfway line for the kick off, went around to each and every player to remind them of their responsibilities.

Born: Rio de Janeiro, 8th October 1929
Died: 12th May 2001
Debut: Brazil v Mexico, 6/4/1952
Appearances: 68 caps for Brazil
Honours: Carioca champion (1951, 1957, 1961, 1962), World Cup winner (1958, 1962).
Current Status: Deceased

Legends of **FOOTBALL**

LEFT
Didi tries to get past Hungarian full-back Mihaly Lantos during the 1954 World Cup.

BELOW
Didi practising his heading skills.

assistance or support from his so-called team-mates. In desperation he went out on loan to Valencia but when that failed to work out he begged Real Madrid to tear up his contract so he could return home to Brazil.

Whilst Real Madrid may not have wanted him, he went straight back into the Botafogo side and helped them win the championship in 1961 and 1962. That latter year also saw him collect a second World Cup winners' medal as Brazil overcame Czechoslovakia, without the injured Pelé, proof that Didi was probably the more vital member of the side at the time. Far more satisfying however, was a 2-1 victory over Spain in the group stages, with Puskas and Gento, his former Real Madrid team-mates, part of the Spanish side that finished bottom of the group and heading for an early elimination (Di Stefano was injured just before the World Cup finals and took no part in the competition).

After the World Cup, Didi took up the position of player-coach at Sporting Cristal in Peru, guiding them to runners-up spot in their domestic League. He finished his playing career with Sao Paolo in 1966 and then turned to coaching, unearthing such talent as Hector Chumpitaz and Teofilo Cubillas and guiding Peru to the World Cup quarter-finals in 1970, the first time they had qualified before they lost to eventual winners Brazil. He later moved to Europe, taking Fenerbahce to the Turkish Super Ligi in 1974 and 1975.

His performances in Sweden attracted the attentions of Real Madrid, who paid £30,000 to take him to Spain in October 1959 to bolster a side that already boasted the talents of Puskas and Alfredo Di Stefano. Although Didi was widely regarded as one of the best players in the world, there were bigger egos at Real Madrid than he had come up against elsewhere and he played no part in the European Cup conquests and received virtually no

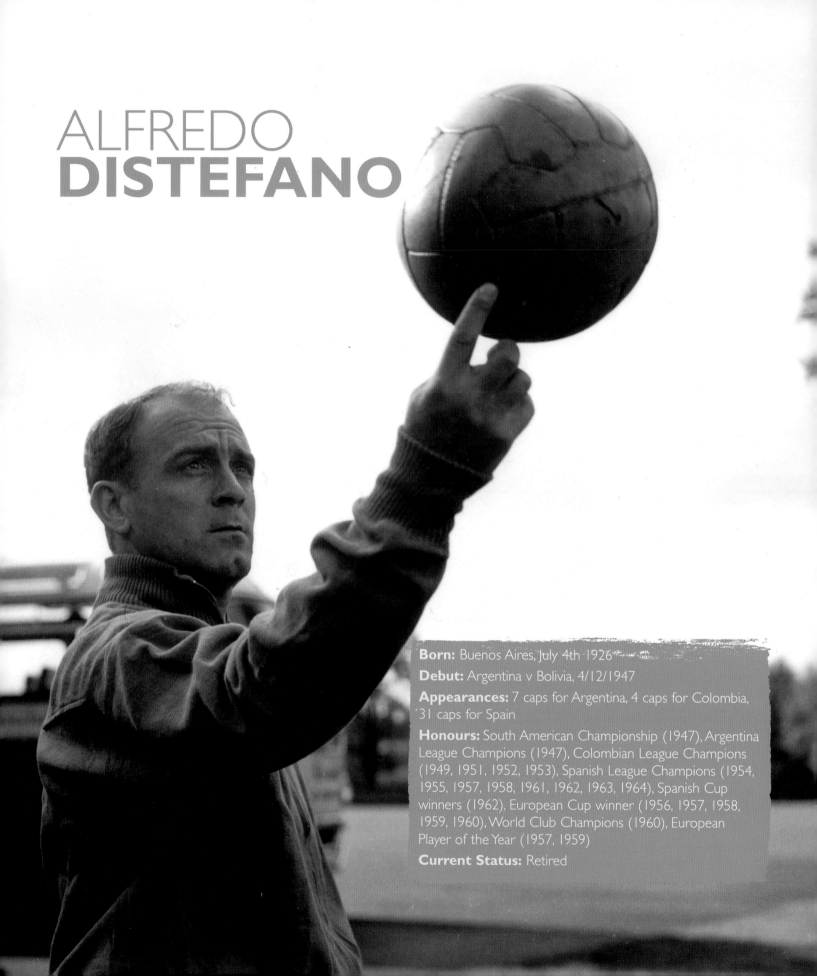

ALFREDO
DISTEFANO

Born: Buenos Aires, July 4th 1926

Debut: Argentina v Bolivia, 4/12/1947

Appearances: 7 caps for Argentina, 4 caps for Colombia, 31 caps for Spain

Honours: South American Championship (1947), Argentina League Champions (1947), Colombian League Champions (1949, 1951, 1952, 1953), Spanish League Champions (1954, 1955, 1957, 1958, 1961, 1962, 1963, 1964), Spanish Cup winners (1962), European Cup winner (1956, 1957, 1958, 1959, 1960), World Club Champions (1960), European Player of the Year (1957, 1959)

Current Status: Retired

Real Madrid was formed in 1902 and had a largely undistinguished first fifty years, not even being considered the best club in Spain, let alone the best in Europe. All that was to change with the acquisition of Alfredo Di Stefano in 1953, perhaps the player who became most responsible for the club's elevation to becoming the biggest in the world.

Alfredo was born in Buenos Aires in 1926 the son of Italian parents who owned a farm just outside of the city. As the eldest son of the family, Alfredo had to do much of the work on the farm, which enabled him to build up his stamina, whilst playing youth football with Los Cardales. He was subsequently spotted by River Plate, playing initially in the reserves before earning a place in the first team at the age of 16.

Although he had played at centre forward in his youth and would go on to make the position his at his subsequent clubs, Alfredo was initially used as a right winger and then sent on loan to Huracan, returning to River Plate when the club sold the great Pedernera to Atlanta. He made an immediate impact, helping the club win the Argentinean League in 1947 and finishing top goalscorer with 27 goals in 30 matches as well as earning a call up into the Argentine national side. That same year came the Copa America, with Alfredo being drafted into the side after Pontoni suffered an injury and finished second top goalscorer as Argentina won the competition.

A strike over wages in 1949 prompted many players to head elsewhere in search of professional football, with Alfredo joining Millionarios of Colombia. As Colombia were not members of FIFA, no transfer fee was paid and Alfredo received considerably higher wages than he might otherwise have expected. Alfredo was just as successful in Colombia as he had been in his native Argentina, netting 267 goals in 292 appearances and winning four League Championship medals, including three in consecutive seasons. He even got to make four appearances for the Colombian national side, even though he had been previously capped by Argentina.

In 1953 Millionarios made a brief European tour, including a visit to Spain to take on Real Madrid as part of Real's fiftieth anniversary celebrations. Alfredo Di Stefano helped Millionarios win Real's tournament and alerted the top Spanish clubs as to his abilities, with Barcelona contacting River Plate of Argentina, who still officially held his playing registration, to try and secure

BELOW

Di Stefano (centre) helps collect the European Cup for Real Madrid in 1959.

his services. Real Madrid did likewise and at one point Alfredo was officially linked to both Barcelona and Real Madrid. An initial suggestion that both clubs share the player was discounted, as was Barcelona's suggestion that they should both relinquish their interest and sell him to Juventus. Eventually Real were able to buy the player outright for £70,000, a very small price to pay for the glories Alfredo was to bring.

Alfredo slotted into the Real side immediately, linking with Francisco Gento to form the backbone of the side that would dominate Europe for the next five or six years. Real Madrid won the Spanish League in 1954 and retained it twelve months later, giving them entry to the newly created European Champion Clubs Cup, or European Cup as it became more commonly known. Aggregate victories over Servette, Partizan Belgrade and AC Milan took them into the final to face Stade De Reims, a formidable French side led by Raymond Kopa. On the day however Real Madrid in general and Alfredo Di Stefano in particular had too much ability and came from behind twice to finally win 4-3 in Paris.

The history books show that Real Madrid were to retain the trophy for the next four years, beating Fiorentina 2-0 in 1957, AC Milan 3-2 in 1958, Stade De Reims again 2-0 in 1959 and Eintracht Frankfurt 7-3 in 1960. The history books, however, only tell part of the story, for Alfredo Di Stefano scored in all five of Real's finals, an astonishing feat in itself. The last of these victories, a 7-3 win over Eintracht that saw Alfredo net a hat-trick is widely regarded as one the greatest club performances of all time, with Real's attack boasting the

dual talents of Alfredo Di Stefano and Ferenc Puskas
(who scored the other four goals on the night).

Indeed, it was Real's European successes that enabled
them to grow stronger with each passing season, with
the revenues generated being used to strengthen the side
on a regular basis, with Puskas and Kopa joining the
club before the decade was out.

No matter who arrived, the key player was still
Alfredo Di Stefano, whose tactical awareness, eye for
goal and overall vision made him the playmaker within
the side. Alfredo even earned representative honours
with Spain, the third and final country he represented
during his long career, but the one thing that eluded
him, irrespective of who he played for was an
appearance at the World Cup – Alfredo Di Stefano made
his impact on the club front, netting a then record 49
goals in 58 European matches for Real, a record that was
finally beaten by Raul of Real in 2005.

He remained a player at Real Madrid until 1964,
helping Real reach two further European Cup finals
although both of these ended in defeat. He then signed
for Espanol before hanging up his boots at the age of 40
in 1966.

Alfredo then went into coaching and management,
taking Boca Juniors and River Plate to the Argentine
League title and winning the Spanish League, Spanish
Cup and European Cup Winners' Cup with Valencia.

He had a brief spell in charge at his beloved Real
Madrid too, between 1982 and 1984 but was
unsuccessful in his attempts to being back the glory
days. There again, who could hope to emulate five
consecutive European Cup triumphs. No matter who
was in charge of Real Madrid, the one thing they could
never replace or repeat was the ability of Alfredo Di
Stefano, a player many consider at least the equal of Pelé
in his prime.

DUNCAN EDWARDS

Duncan Edwards was fated to enjoy a professional career of just five years but did enough in that very short space of time to earn himself the moniker of legend. There are many who feel that but for the Munich air disaster, which ultimately was to cost Duncan his life, he would have gone on to become one of the greatest players the world has ever seen, such was the esteem in which he was held.

A member of the school sides at Priory Primary School and Wolverhampton Street Secondary School, Duncan's performances earned him selection for the England schoolboy side in 1950, where he came under the tutelage of former England international Joe Mercer. Having seen him play on a number of occasions, Mercer was in no doubt as to Duncan's future and tipped off Manchester United manager Matt Busby as to his abilities. Busby duly despatched chief scout Joe Armstrong to check for himself – Armstrong needed just ten minutes to confirm Mercer's observation.

Matt Busby and his assistant Jimmy Murphy continued watching Duncan for the next two years and made sure he signed for Manchester United on his sixteenth birthday, virtually camping outside his house in order to sign him as soon after midnight as possible! Within six months Duncan had made his League debut, making him the then youngest player to make his First Division debut, and two years later, on 2nd April 1955 against Scotland he became England's youngest post-war debutant, a record he held until overtaken by the likes of Wayne Rooney and Theo Woolcott.

Such were his all-round abilities, even those who played with or against him or were fortunate enough to have seen him play disagree on his strengths (he had virtually no weaknesses). Although he played as a wing half, he popped up in a variety of positions around the field as play dictated, able to dribble his way out of trouble from the wing, set up chances for the centre forward from an inside forward position and tackle like a full back. He was as strong as an ox, meaning he was extremely difficult to knock off the ball, but had all the composure going when a cool head was needed.

Undoubtedly the major star of the so-called Busby Babes, Duncan was an integral part of the side that won the FA Youth Cup in 1953, 1954 and 1955 (the first three years the competition was staged, and United would retain the trophy for a further two years as a succession of top quality players came off the United conveyor belt), even though he was also a virtual first team regular throughout the same period.

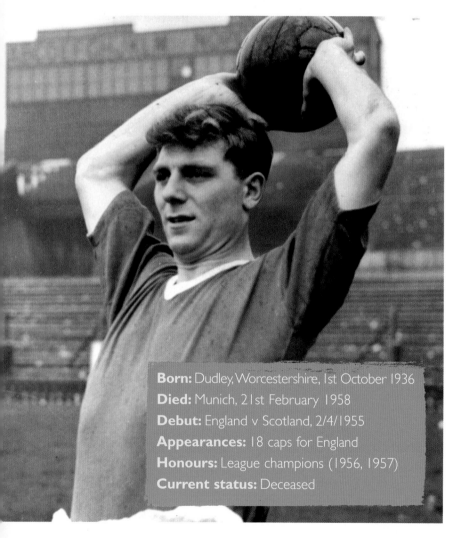

Born: Dudley, Worcestershire, 1st October 1936
Died: Munich, 21st February 1958
Debut: England v Scotland, 2/4/1955
Appearances: 18 caps for England
Honours: League champions (1956, 1957)
Current status: Deceased

the accident, but he eventually began to bleed internally. Two weeks later, longer than anyone had expected, Duncan finally lost his greatest battle. He was just 22 years of age.

Whilst the loss to Manchester United was immeasurable (the club would not win the League again for a further seven years), England suffered too. Duncan had won 18 caps by the time of his death and was as vital to the national side as he was to his club. England had a miserable World Cup in 1958 and were not much better four years later. In 1966, when they won the competition on home turf, many were convinced that but for Munich, it would have been Duncan Edwards climbing the steps towards the Royal Box to collect the trophy, not Bobby Moore. Because of Munich, we will never know.

Matt Busby never had any doubts about Duncan Edwards. Of all the players he lost at Munich, virtually all of them internationals he had nurtured through the ranks, he felt the loss of Duncan most. 'The best player in the world' was his simple description. He was buried at Dudley Cemetery five days after his death and is honoured with a stained glass window at the Priory Church in the town, with football fans regularly making something of a pilgrimage to locate both.

LEFT
Duncan Edwards in action, just one month before the Munich air disaster.

BELOW
Stained glass window at St. Francis' Church in Dudley, commemorating Duncan Edwards.

Duncan would go on to help the United first team win the League title in 1956, thus earning them their first tilt at the European Cup. The following season therefore saw United competing on three fronts, retaining the League, reaching the European Cup semi-final and narrowly missing out on the double when they were beaten by Aston Villa in the FA Cup final. That League title, however, was enough to put United back into the premier European club competition.

United had secured their place in the semi finals with an aggregate victory over Red Star Belgrade and were returning home when the plane made a refuelling stop in Munich. After two unsuccessful attempts at take off the plane's third attempt saw it slam into a building at the end of the runway, killing seven of his team-mates immediately. Duncan was severely injured, having had his kidneys crushed but, such was his strength, he battled for life for a further two weeks. An artificial kidney was rushed to the hospital the day after

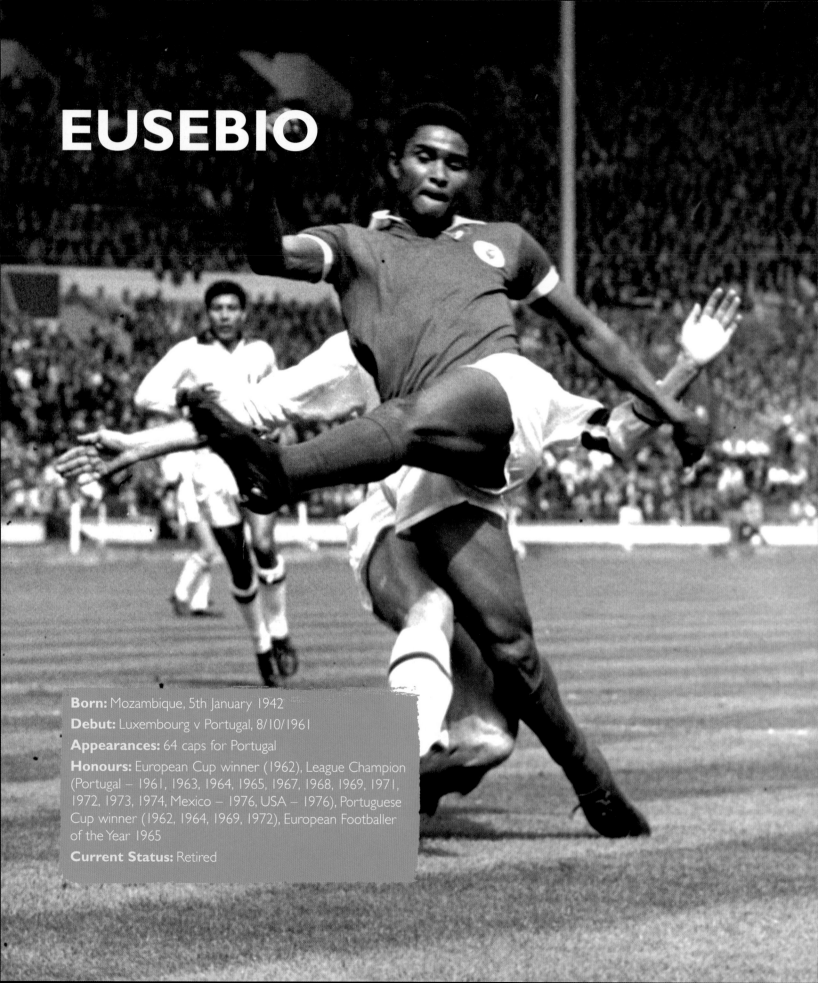

EUSEBIO

Born: Mozambique, 5th January 1942

Debut: Luxembourg v Portugal, 8/10/1961

Appearances: 64 caps for Portugal

Honours: European Cup winner (1962), League Champion (Portugal – 1961, 1963, 1964, 1965, 1967, 1968, 1969, 1971, 1972, 1973, 1974, Mexico – 1976, USA – 1976), Portuguese Cup winner (1962, 1964, 1969, 1972), European Footballer of the Year 1965

Current Status: Retired

Born in 1942 in Lourenço Marques, now in Maputo but then in Mozambique, Eusebio is one of the greatest goalscorers of all time, netting a tally in Portugal that may stand for all time. Many of his goals, especially in the early part of his career, were scored thanks to his lightning burst of pace and it was no surprise to learn that he was the Under 19 Portuguese Champion at the 100, 200 and 400 metres; there was no one who could catch him over ten yards on a football field!

He began his career with his local club Sporting Club of Lourenço Marques and soon attracted attention from bigger clubs. Although Lourenço Marques was a nursery club of Sporting Lisbon, Benfica enviously eyed the young Eusebio and spirited him away to an Algarve fishing village until the arguments between the two clubs died down. Eusebio then joined Benfica of Lisbon for a paltry £7,500 in 1961, a figure that was ridiculously low since he won his first cap for Portugal the same year! His impact with Benfica was no less immediate, helping them win the League Championship at the end of the season and watch them overcome Barcelona in the European Cup final the same month. Eusebio got his reward twelve months later, being part of the side that overcame Real Madrid 5-3 in one of the great finals to retain the European Cup, with Eusebio netting two of Benfica's goals.

That proved to be the pinnacle of Benfica's European accomplishments, for the holders were beaten in the final of 1963 against AC Milan at Wembley. Wembley was not to be the happiest of hunting grounds for Eusebio, for there was a further defeat at the grand old stadium in 1968 against Manchester United, which itself came three years after Benfica had lost to the other Milan side, Internazionale in Milan itself.

On the domestic front Benfica were virtually without rival, winning eleven League titles out of fourteen and the Portuguese Cup on four occasions. Thanks to Eusebio, Portugal also improved their world standing, finishing third in the 1966 World Cup finals in England, where Eusebio finished the tournament top goalscorer with nine goals, including four in an astonishing match against North Korea that Portugal finally won 5-3 after being three goals behind. It was his performances during that competition that proved he was worthy of the monikers bestowed upon him, being known as the Black Pearl and the Black Panther.

EUSEBIO

Awarded the accolade of European Footballer of the Year in 1965, Eusebio was also the inaugural winner of the Golden Boot Award in 1968 as Europe's leading goalscorer. He was top goalscorer in Portugal every year from 1964 to 1973 and repeated his Golden Boot Award in 1973. By the time he left Benfica in 1975, he had scored 727 goals in 715 matches for the club! His goalscoring record for his country was no less impressive, resulting in a tally of 41 goals in 62 matches, a record that stood until Pauleta equalled it in 2004.

After a spell playing for lesser Portuguese teams Beira-Mar and União de Tomar (he only scored six goals for the two sides!) he headed across the Atlantic and played for the Boston Minutemen and Toronto Metros-Croatia, where he won a US Soccer Bowl medal before

heading to Mexico to play for CF Monterrey. He made ten appearances, enough to help them win their League Championship and earn yet another medal for himself!

Eusebio returned to America in 1977 and played briefly for Las Vegas Quicksilvers. Unfortunately, Eusebio was not quite as quick as the 'Silvers required and with his knees beginning to play up, he decided to call it a day that same year, although he did attempt a comeback the following year with New Jersey Americans in the Second Division.

Like many of his generation, such as Bobby Charlton at Manchester United and Franz Beckenbauer at Bayern Munich, the name of Eusebio is synonymous with that of one club, Benfica, and he continues to serve the club in an off the field capacity. It is a different Benfica to the

one that Eusebio graced as a player, one that has been replaced at the pinnacle of Portuguese football by the likes of FC Porto. Since Eusebio left the club in 1975, Benfica have appeared in just two European finals, the UEFA Cup in 1983 and the European Cup in 1990 and lost them both.

The Portuguese national side has similarly struggled to replace the goalscoring abilities of Eusebio, with the result that they have made only occasional appearances on the world stage since those heady days of 1966. Despite this, Eusebio is often used as an inspirational character before international matches, his legend and status enough to earn him a standing ovation more than thirty years after he left the stage he most certainly graced.

LUIS**FIGO**

Luis Figo is one of a select band of players who has played for both Barcelona and Real Madrid, with his switch from the former to the latter in 2000 inflaming an already volatile rivalry. Indeed, the Barcelona fans were opposed to his transfer so vehemently they were still protesting about it in 2004!

Born in Lisbon in 1972 Luis began his career with Sporting Club de Portugal, rising through the club's ranks and representing Portugal at Under 16 and Under 20 level and helping them win the FIFA World Youth Championship in 1991. Alongside Rui Costa he was seen as one of the golden generation of Portuguese players, an exciting midfield player around which Portugal would build a formidable side. He was capped at full level at the age of 18 and would go on to be regular in the side for the next fifteen years, a brief spell resting notwithstanding.

After helping Sporting Club de Portugal to the Portuguese cup in 1995 there was speculation that he was bound for Italy and duly signed contracts with both Juventus and Parma, which resulted in a two-year ban on any move to Italy! Instead he moved to Spain, signing for Johan Cruyff and Barcelona. An instant favourite at the Nou Camp he helped the club win the Spanish League in 1998 and 1999, the Copa Del Rey in 1997 and 1998 and the European Cup Winners' Cup in 1997, adding the European Super Cup in 1998, with Luis club captain for most of these successes.

His eventual move to Real Madrid in 2000 for a then world record fee of £38.7 million provoked outrage at the Nou Camp, especially after Luis himself had discounted any move to the Bernabeu. Luis went from being an idol of Barcelona to public enemy number one, with websites being set up for the sole purpose of displaying insults against their former star. Luis missed his first planned return to the Nou Camp owing to injury – when he finally played in 2002 the ground was nearly shut down after an assortment of objects, including a pig's head were thrown at him. In 2004, four years after he had left the club, a Barcelona fan invaded the pitch during the 2004 European Championships in Portugal and threw a Barcelona flag at a bemused Luis Figo!

Born: Lisbon, 4th November 1972

Debut: Portugal v Luxembourg, 16/10/1991

Appearances: 127 caps for Portugal

Honours: Portuguese Cup winners (1995), Copa Del Rey winners (1997, 1998), Spanish champions (1998, 1999, 2001, 2003), European Cup Winners' Cup winner (1997), UEFA Champions League winner (2002), European Super Cup winner (1998, 2002), Intercontinental Cup winner (2002), Italian League champion (2006), Coppa Italia winner (2006), Italian Super Cup winner (2005, 2006)

Current Status: Still playing

Legends of **FOOTBALL**

Luis and Zinedine exchanged shirts and pleasantries, with Zinedine going off to prepare for the final and Luis for the third and fourth-place play-off. He came off the bench in the 77th minute to make his 127th and final appearance for Portugal but could not help them overcome the Germans, although fourth place represented their best performance since 1966. His international career had seen him score a more than healthy 32 goals, a welcome return for a midfield player.

The end to his Real Madrid career came in 2005 and he moved to Italy (at last!) on a free transfer to join Inter Milan. He helped them win the Italian Cup and, after finishing third in the League behind Juventus and AC Milan were subsequently awarded the championship after the match fixing scandal saw AC, Juventus, Lazio and Fiorentina docked points.

Named European Footballer of the Year in 2000 and FIFA World Player of the Year in 2001, Luis has interests outside of football, linking with Manchester United assistant coach Carlos Queiroz to work with A1 Grand Prix Team Portugal and its driver Alvaro Parente.

Luis Figo has made nearly five hundred appearances for his four clubs, scoring 89 goals. It is the number of chances he created for others that have made his reputation however, as well as a place in the FIFA list of Top 100 players.

What probably rankled most was that at Real Madrid Luis Figo showed why he was so highly rated as a player, being one of the major stars in a side that bristled with talent in every position. Alongside Zinedine Zidane, Roberto Carlos, Ronaldo and Raul, Luis Figo helped Real win the UEFA Champions League in 2002, earning them the moniker of the Greatest Club in the World. Either side of this victory were successes in the Spanish League, taking to 29 the number of titles won by Real Madrid. Whilst Real Madrid were a good side prior to his arrival, with him in midfield they became a great one.

After helping Portugal to the final of the European Championships in 2004, Luis announced his temporary retirement from international duty, returning in April 2005 to help Portugal qualify for the 2006 World Cup in Germany. There he inspired his country to the semi-final stage before being beaten by France by a Zinedine Zidane penalty, although Luis had a chance to level but headed over. At the end of the game former team-mates

TOM**FINNEY**

Born: Preston, 5th April 1922
Debut: Northern Ireland v England, 28/9/1946
Appearances: 76 caps for England
Honours: Player of the Year (1954, 1957)
Current Status: Retired

Legends aren't always measured by the number of medals they won. There are many players who have won all the honours the game has to offer yet still aren't classed as legends, mainly because they all too often put their own needs above those of the team. Tom Finney won next to nothing in the game but fully deserves to be considered a legend, simply because he always put the team's interests ahead of his own.

Born just across the road from Deepdale, Tom suffered from an infected gland at the age of six and was required to attend hospital twice a week for the next eight years until the gland was finally removed. At that point Tom was 14, stood just 4' 9" tall and weighed five stone, yet he was still considered good enough to be invited along for a trial with Preston North End. He did well enough to be offered a place on the ground staff for ten shillings a week, playing junior football and undertaking the usual ground duties of cleaning boots and sweeping the terrace. Although Tom had set his heart on becoming a player, his father advised him to continue his apprenticeship as a plumber and join Preston as an amateur. That way if it didn't work out for him as a player, he would have a trade to fall back on.

Tom was at Wembley to watch Preston win the FA Cup final in 1938, the last major honour the club won. Two years later Tom was offered professional terms with the club and made his debut in the war-time League, going on to help the club win the Northern Section and the Wartime Cup, beating Arsenal 2-1 in a replay at Ewood Park – it would be the only final of his career that Tom actually won!

Tom was called up as a trooper in the Royal Armoured Corps in 1942 and eventually served in the Eighth Army as a tank driver and mechanic during the war, although he also found time to turn out for Newcastle, Southampton and Bolton as a guest as well as Preston before the war came to a close.

He was de-mobbed quickly after the hostilities came to an end, his profession of plumber being a much needed occupation, which enabled him to rejoin Preston at the same time. Tom was also invited along for the FA tour of Switzerland in 1945, appearing in both matches against the hosts and scoring one of the goals in the 3-0 victory in the second match. Although these have never been classified as full internationals, all of the players on the trip were English and contemporary pictures show the side to be wearing the distinctive three lions badge – Tom Finney is therefore one of a select band of players who made his international debut before he made his official League debut.

That eventually came when League football was resumed in 1946, and a couple of weeks later Tom was given the first of his 76 official caps for his country, scoring one of England's goals in the 7-2 win over Northern Ireland. That match had seen Tom play at right wing, a position that had previously been the almost exclusive preserve of Stan Matthews, but Tom proved not only a more than adequate replacement on the day but a player who was equally indispensable to the side – the selectors eventually worked out a way to accommodate both Tom Finney and Stan Matthews in the same team.

Therein lay the secret, if it was indeed a secret, of Tom's abilities – of his 76 caps, 40 of them came playing on the right wing, 33 on the left wing and the remaining three as an emergency centre forward. Whilst Stan Matthews concentrated almost solely on fashioning chances for others, Tom Finney could be relied upon to grab his fair share, netting 30 during the course of his international career. Burnley and Northern Ireland international Jimmy McIlroy described him 'As a right-winger converted from a left footer, he was the best centre-forward I've ever seen!'

Tom appeared in three World Cup tournaments, 1950, 1954 and 1958 and made his final appearance for his country in the 5-0 friendly win over Russia in 1958. Although his international career came to an end, Tom was still a vital player for Preston. Indeed, he was often more than vital, for in the season he was out for a lengthy spell with injury, Preston got relegated.

With Tom's help Preston bounced straight back as Second Division Champions in 1950-51, the only medal Tom won during his career. He did help them reach the FA Cup final in 1954, with most of the country

fee to Preston for their inconvenience too. Preston and Tom turned them down.

Tom remained a player at Preston until his retirement in 1960 – a year later Preston were relegated and haven't been back to the top flight since. Tom was lured out of retirement in 1963, receiving a call from Distillery manager George Eastham and agreeing to play in the home leg of a European Cup tie against Benfica. Distillery, inspired by Tom Finney, raised their game to undreamed of heights and recorded a 3-3 draw.

Never booked, sent off or even spoken to by a referee during his career, Tom was awarded the OBE in 1961. He continued his plumbing business in the town of Preston, served as a magistrate, chairman of the local health authority and President of Preston North End football club. He was knighted in 1998, again for his services to football. He may not have won much from the game, but he gave it everything – he is a true legend.

expecting Tom to influence Preston in much the same way Stan Matthews had at Blackpool twelve months previously, but West Bromwich Albion skipper Len Millard kept him quiet and with no one else to orchestrate matters, Preston went down 3-2 on the day.

His performances for Preston often attracted interest from elsewhere, but with the maximum wage in force and a thriving business as a plumber in Preston, there was no point in going elsewhere. One offer did come in from abroad, Palermo of Italy offering a £10,000 signing on fee, wages of £130 a month, bonuses of £100 a game, a villa on the Mediterranean, a car and free travel to and from Italy for him and his family, and a £30,000

JUSTFONTAINE

The majority of the entrants in this book of football legends earned their place thanks to their exploits over an entire career, with varying degrees of success. Just Fontaine owes much of his reputation thanks to six matches in one World Cup competition, but his tally of thirteen goals set a record that is unlikely to be broken in a single competition.

Born in Morocco, Just began his career with USM Casablanca in 1950 and spent three years with the club before moving to France (Morocco was then a colony of France) to join Nice in 1953. In three seasons with Nice he scored 44 goals, an impressive tally that earned him a call up for the French national side in December 1953, with Just scoring a hat-trick in the 8-0 rout of Luxembourg.

With Raymond Kopa bound for Real Madrid after the 1956 European Cup Final, Stade De Reims saw Just Fontaine as the ideal replacement and swooped to secure his signature in time for the 1956-57 season.

It proved to be an inspired choice, for over the next six seasons Just would make 200 appearances and score 165 goals, enabling the club to win the League title in 1958 and 1960 and the French Cup in 1958. In 1959 he helped them reach the final of the European Cup, but again they came up against an inspired Real Madrid who made sure of their fourth consecutive European Cup with a 2-0 victory.

By then Just Fontaine was something of a celebrity beyond France, thanks to his exploits the previous summer in Sweden in the World Cup. France had struggled to qualify and had not won a match since September 1957. They set up a training camp in Sweden a month before any of the other competing countries arrived, prompting some unkind comments from their own media that they had arrived early because they would be departing early!

Like many players, Just was superstitious enough to insist on using an old pair of boots, but these fell apart during one training session before the competition had even kicked off. They were the only pair of boots Just had taken to the competition (most players of this era had only one or two pairs and sponsors were very much a thing of the future!), but fortunately team-mate Stephane Bruey had similar sized feet and lent Just his spare pair.

Born: Marrakech, Morocco, 18th August 1933
Debut: France v Luxembourg, 17/12/1953
Appearances: 21 caps for France
Honours: French champions (1958, 1960), French Cup winner (1958)
Current Status: Retired

The effects of a month-long team bonding found the French able to play above themselves during the competition, and no one benefited more than Just Fontaine. He netted three in the opening match against Paraguay in a 7-3 win and got both French goals in a 3-2 defeat by Yugoslavia. France made sure of further progress with a 2-1 victory over Scotland in their final group match, with Just netting one of the goals. In the quarter-final against Northern Ireland he scored twice in a 4-0 win, putting the French into the semi-final to face Brazil. Just equalised Brazil's opening goal and the match seemed set to be an intriguing affair, but soon after French captain Robert Jonquet suffered a fractured fibula and France had to play for almost an hour with only ten men (there were no substitutes in those days). Brazil made the extra man advantage count to the full, finally winning 5-2 on their way to registering a similar score in the final against the hosts Sweden. There were even more goals in the third and fourth place play off between France and holders West Germany, with France winning an open match 6-3 and with Just netting four of France's goals to give him a tally of

thirteen for the competition. According to Just, he handed back the boots to Stephane Bruey and commented 'So many of my goals were inspired by the presence of two spirits within one sole.'

Just returned to Stade De Reims and helped them win the League title again in 1960. He seemed set to continue scoring for both his club and country but for a double fracture of his left leg during a match against Sochaux in the run in for the 1959-60 season. Ten months later he returned to action but suffered a repeat fracture and was forced to retire at the age of just 27. His 21 international appearances for France had brought him an astonishing 30 goals, but it is the thirteen scored in the World Cup that set him apart – a record tally in a single competition, it was not overtaken at all until Gerd Muller netted the fourteen of his World Cup career in 1974. In 2006, Ronaldo netted the fifteenth goal of his three World Cup finals to take the overall lead.

Just Fontaine's accomplishments in Sweden in 1958 have never been forgotten in France, leading him to be selected France's greatest living player. He still receives twenty or so letter a week from fans, more than 48 years after the event. That makes him a true legend.

GARRINCHA

One of the most talented of players on the field, Garrincha established an equally formidable reputation off it, having fathered at least 14 children before his death at the age of forty-nine.

Born Manuel Francisco Dos Santos in the Pau Grande district of Mage in the state of Rio de Janeiro, he was given the nickname Garrincha, which means 'songbird' on account of his love of the bird. He was born with deformed legs, with his left leg bent inwards and his right leg six centimetres shorter and bent outwards. This meant a number of operations as a child in an attempt to correct the deformity and whilst the condition improved it was never fully corrected, although it never interfered with his abilities as a footballer.

Garrincha grew up playing football in the streets of his hometown and developed his amazing dribbling skills along the way. Often he did not have a ball to play with, kicking a rolled up sock and other improvised spherical objects during childhood and not having regular use of a proper ball until he went into the professional game.

He began his career with his local Pau Grande club and signed with the Botafogo club in 1953. Although he looked ungainly, especially with his pronounced deformity, Garrincha made an immediate impact at the club, knocking the ball through the legs of Nilton Santos, an established Brazilian international at the club. After a brief starring role for the reserves Garrincha was drafted in to the first team and became one of the stars of the Botafogo side, although it was not enough to earn him a call up into the Brazilian World Cup squad for the 1954 finals in Switzerland.

Brazil's somewhat lack-lustre performance in Switzerland (they went out at the quarter-final stage) had the media and public alike calling for changes to the side and Garrincha was handed an international debut in 1955. After helping Botafogo win the Carioca League Championship, Garrincha virtually guaranteed himself a place in the World Cup squad for 1958 in Sweden.

Garrincha didn't feature in either of the two opening matches, a 3-0 win over Austria and a goalless draw with England but was drafted into the side for the vital third match against the Russians, which Brazil ultimate won 2-0 to book their place in the quarter-final. This was the start of the 4-4-2 line-up that was to so enthral the world, with Garrincha linking especially well with Pelé (Brazil never lost a single match when Garrincha and Pelé were both on the field) as Wales and France were eased out of the competition and Brazil sailed into the final against Sweden. Whilst Pelé ultimately took the accolades, the contribution of Garrincha should not be overlooked, weaving his magic down the wing twice to

Born: Pau Grande, 28th October 1933
Died: January 20th 1983
Debut: Brazil v Chile, 18/9/1955
Appearances: 60 caps for Brazil
Honours: Carioca League Champion (1957, 1961, 1962), Rio-Sao Paulo Champion (1962, 1964), World Cup winner (1958, 1962)
Current Status: Deceased

Legends of **FOOTBALL**

LEFT
Garrincha bumps into French goalkeeper Claude Abbes during the World Cup semi-final between Brazil and France in Stockholm, 1958.

BELOW
Garrincha helps carry the flag of Sweden, after Brazil beat them to win the World Cup in 1958.

cross for Vava to score, bringing Brazil back from behind on their way to a 5-2 victory.

The history books show that Garrincha won a second winners' medal four years later in Chile, but there was considerable controversy surrounding Garrincha long before a ball was kicked in the competition. His problems began almost as soon as the World Cup winners touched down in Brazil in 1958, with Garrincha piling on the pounds owing to his love of sweets. He was also drinking heavily and was eventually dropped from the Brazil side as they considered him unreliable. Worse was to follow, for just a year after wowing the Swedish nation with his displays on the field in the World Cup, Garrincha returned to the country as part of the touring Botafogo side and got a local girl pregnant, ensuring a different set of headlines.

On his return home he ran over his father and drove off without stopping, being chased by an angry mob. When they finally caught up with him, he was found to be so drunk at the wheel of the car, he had no recollection of what he had done. That August his wife gave birth to the couple's fifth child, the same month his mistress announced her first pregnancy! Football appeared to be the furthest thing from Garrincha's mind!

He eventually got down to some serious training and managed to force his way back into the Brazilian side and was named in the World Cup squad for 1962. With Pelé suffering a torn muscle two games into the competition, Garrincha became even more vital to the side and responded with a series of performances that propelled Brazil into the final. His best performance came in the later stages, netting twice in the quarter-final against England and again in the semi-final against host nation Chile to book Brazil's place in the final, but Garrincha's place in the side was in some considerable doubt owing to the fact he got himself sent off late in the game against Chile. It took a special meeting of FIFA to decide that his sending off would be overlooked and he could play in the match against Czechoslovakia, helping the holders retain the trophy with a 3-1 victory.

Garrincha appeared in the next World Cup in 1966 in England, but it was not an experience remembered with any great pride by many Brazilians, whose grip on the trophy was loosened with successive defeats against Hungary and Portugal. Garrincha's international career came to an end during the competition having made 60 appearances for his country – 52 were won, seven were drawn and only one, that last appearance against Hungary, was lost.

Whilst his international career ended in 1966, Garrincha remained a professional player until 1972, taking in Corinthians, Portuguesa, Flamengo and Olaria in Brazil and Atletico Junior in Colombia. Yet despite this, he was largely ignored and forgotten when he retired. A twice World Cup winner, Garrincha simply didn't know what to do with himself when he left football and spent most of his time drinking in an attempt to forget mounting domestic and tax problems. Eventually alcohol was to kill him at the shockingly early age of 49, just as it had done to his father. His epitaph reads 'Here rests in peace the one who was the Joy of the People – Mané Garrincha'.

FRANCISCO**GENTO**

Whilst the likes of Alfredo Di Stefano and later Ferenc Puskas gained most of the plaudits, for many the engine room of the great Real Madrid side of the 1950s was Francisco Gento. The lively Spaniard outlasted both Di Stefano and Puskas and set a record that is unlikely to be beaten – he won the European Cup a total of six times and appeared in eight finals, all with the same club.

Born in Guarnizo in October 1933 he began his playing career with Racing Santander in 1952. He made just ten appearances for the club, scoring twice, before he switched to Real Madrid where a truly great side was being assembled. Although the side was almost entirely built around the mercurial talents of Alfredo Di Stefano, who scored most of the goals that would enable the club to lift the European Cup five times in succession, it was Francisco Gento that especially made it all possible, creating chance after chance for his team-mates.

Known as La Galerna del Cantabrico (the Storm of the Cantabrico) or El Supersonico, Paco Gento, as he was also known, was an extremely fast and tricky winger, able to beat defenders with ease and could cross the ball with stunning accuracy. It was this ability that first alerted Real Madrid to his abilities and he was seen as the ideal player to play alongside Alfredo Di Stefano, who joined the Madrid giants at roughly the same time.

After winning the Spanish League for the first time in over twenty years in 1954, Real retained it the following year. It was this latter success that ensured qualification for the inaugural European Champion Club's Cup, as the European Cup was officially known. An easy victory over FC Servette was followed by something of a nail-biting clash with Partizan, with Real Madrid winning 4-3 on aggregate despite a 3-0 defeat in Belgrade. After seeing off AC Milan in the semi-final Real had to come from behind before finally beating Stade De Reims in the final 4-3, the first of their five consecutive successes.

History shows Real were to retain the trophy for a further four seasons, with Alfredo Di Stefano scoring in each of the five finals. Whilst he was the man invariably in the right place at the right time to score the goals, the

Born: Guarnizo, 21st October 1933

Debut: Spain v England, 18/5/1955

Appearances: 43 caps for Spain

Honours: Spanish League champions (1954, 1955, 1957, 1958, 1961, 1962, 1963, 1964, 1965, 1967, 1968, 1969), Spanish Cup winners (1962, 1970), European Cup winners (1956, 1957, 1958, 1959, 1960, 1966), Copa Latina winners (1955, 1957), World Club champions (1960)

Current Status: Retired

That brought an end to Paco Gento's playing career having made 517 appearances for Real Madrid and scored 156 goals. He had also made 89 appearances in the European Cup, scoring thirty times. Unfortunately, despite winning a total of 43 caps for Spain between 1955 and 1969, Paco was unable to transfer his domestic success onto the international stage, although he did take part in both the 1962 and 1966 World Cup finals. Spain were eliminated from both tournaments during the group stage, proof that whilst Real Madrid could attract and integrate players from around the world, Spain were still some way short when it came to international matters.

Thus Paco's entire trophy haul came courtesy of Real Madrid – six European Cups, twelve League titles, two Spanish Cups, two Copa Latinas and one World Club championship. At the end of his playing career Paco turned to coaching, having spells with Castilla, Castellon, Palencia and Granada, all of which were spent in the lower leagues. Eventually Paco Gento returned to Real Madrid, serving the club as an ambassador throughout Europe. One of the most loyal and popular players from the 1950s side, it was a post he alone deserved. He was still collecting honours in 2006, being presented with a plaque to commemorate his being the top goalscorer in the Ramon de Carranza Trophy, which he won six times during his spell with Real Madrid.

LEFT
Gento gets past Manchester United's keeper Alex Stepney to score for Real Madrid in the European Cup second leg semi-final, 1968.

BELOW
Francisco Gento with the European Cup after Real Madrid had beaten Partizan Belgrade 2-1 in the final in Brussels, May 1966.

ammunition was provided by Paco Gento, whose forays up and down the left wing created the chances for a hungry Real forward line, Paco could also weigh in vital goals himself, scoring in the 1957 victory over Fiorentina and the winning goal in extra time in the 1958 victory over AC Milan.

After five straight victories Real were beaten in the finals of 1962 and 1964 but returned to the final once again in 1966 where they were to face Partizan again. Although he was not on the scoresheet, Paco had the honour of captaining the side to victory, collecting the trophy after a 2-0 victory. He thus became the first and so far only player to have featured in six European Cup winning sides. Although further success in Europe's premier club competition proved elusive, Paco still featured in another European final, helping Real reach the final of the European Cup Winners' Cup in 1971 against Chelsea. Substituted during the first match, which finished a 1-1 draw, Paco was brought off the bench during the replay in an attempt to rescue a match Real were eventually to lose 2-1.

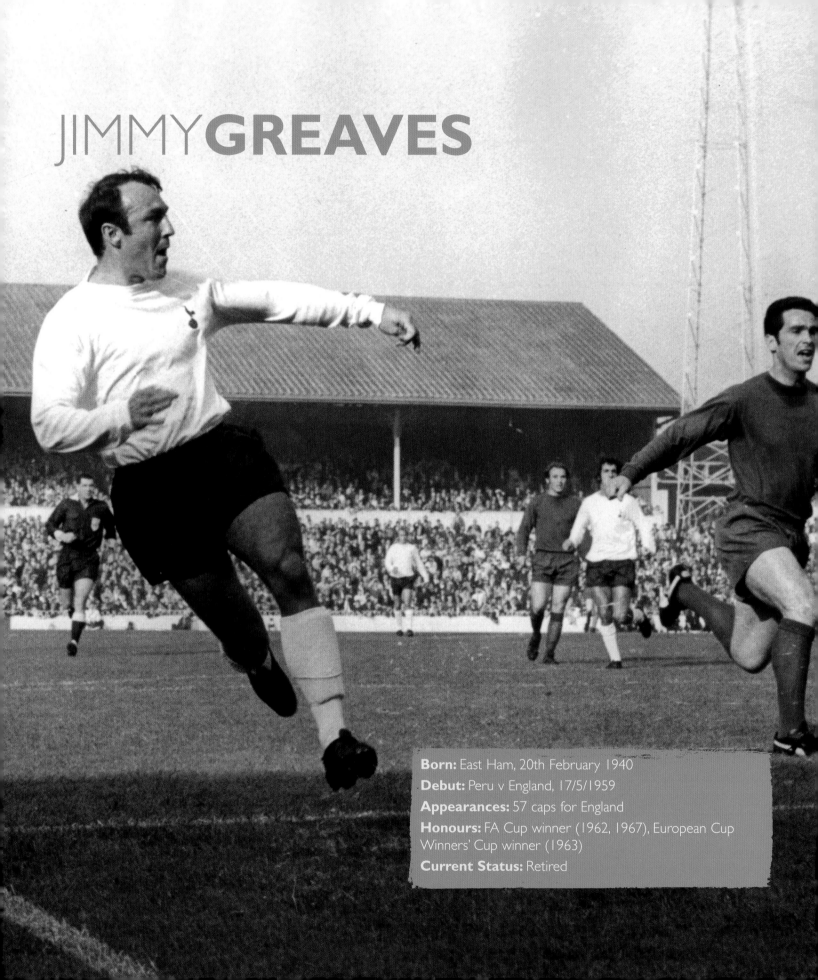

JIMMY**GREAVES**

Born: East Ham, 20th February 1940
Debut: Peru v England, 17/5/1959
Appearances: 57 caps for England
Honours: FA Cup winner (1962, 1967), European Cup Winners' Cup winner (1963)
Current Status: Retired

Jimmy Greaves scored on every one of his debuts – for Chelsea, AC Milan, Tottenham and West Ham at club level and for England at youth, Under 23 and full level but is perhaps best known for the one match he didn't even play in – the 1966 World Cup final.

A phenomenal goalscorer at schoolboy level, Jimmy seemed set to join Spurs from school but instead signed with Chelsea, rattling in scores of goals at junior level. He was given a League debut in 1957 ironically against Spurs and grabbed Chelsea's goal in the 1-1 draw. The step up a level did little to blunt his goalscoring abilities and he finished the League's top goalscorer in 1959 and 1961, with his tally of 41 goals in 1961 remaining Chelsea's club record. In 1960 he became the youngest player to have scored 100 League goals, a feat achieved at just 20 years and 290 days.

With the maximum wage in force during his initial career, Jimmy accepted an offer to join AC Milan in 1961, with Chelsea collecting £80,000 for the player, although by the time the deal went through the maximum wage had been lifted and Chelsea made a concerted effort to back out of the deal, to no avail. Although Jimmy struggled to come to terms with the strict discipline within Italian football, which meant that much of his extra wages went in fines, he did score goals against packed Italian defences, netting 9 in just 14 games. However, continued problems off the field left it very much in everyone's interests that the player return to England, with Chelsea expected to re-sign him. A chance meeting with Spurs manager Bill Nicholson at an awards evening shortly before he had left for Italy had

convinced Nicholson that should the chance arise Jimmy Greaves would like to sign for Spurs, and so Nicholson journeyed to Italy with Chelsea's representative with both trying to sign the proven goalscorer. Nicholson knew Chelsea's ceiling and topped it, although he ended up having to pay £99,999 to get his man – he refused to pay the extra £1 in order that Jimmy wasn't burdened with the tag of being the first £100,000 player.

Jimmy enjoyed the most prolific days of his career at White Hart Lane, scoring 220 goals in 321 games. He topped the goalscoring charts in 1963, 1964, 1965 and 1969, making him the only player to have topped the charts six times, and was the club's top goalscorer in virtually every season at the club, including a record 37 in 1963. He helped Spurs win the FA Cup in 1962 (in which he scored) and 1967 and scored twice in the 1963 European Cup Winners' Cup final to ensure Spurs

became the first British club to win a European trophy.

His goalscoring for England was little less phenomenal – 44 goals in 57 appearances, including a record six hat-tricks. A bout of hepatitis in 1966 restricted him to just 15 goals that season, but he was a member of the England squad for the World Cup finals and appeared in all three group matches, although he didn't score. A gash on his leg kept him out of the quarter-final, with his replacement Geoff Hurst scoring the only goal of the game against Argentina and then retaining his place all the way to the final, in which he scored three goals. Although Jimmy was fit for the final, Alf Ramsey decided against changing the side, although apparently it was Roger Hunt who was most at risk if Ramsey had decided to bring back Jimmy Greaves.

He returned to the side the following year and added one more goal in his final three appearances before ruling himself out of future contention. In 1970 he was sold to West Ham in the same deal that took World Cup winner Martin Peters to White Hart Lane, with Jimmy netting twice on his West Ham debut against Manchester City. That same year he did go to Mexico, although it was as a contestant in the London to Mexico car rally rather than as a member of the World Cup squad – he finished a creditable sixth.

He retired from playing in 1971, ridiculously early for a player of his talents, although he could still be seen playing in the occasional testimonial (he scored in his own testimonial for Spurs against Feyenoord) before

LEFT
Greaves runs onto the pitch for Spurs.

FAR LEFT
Greaves in action for West Ham, 1970.

BELOW
Jimmy Greaves, TV broadcaster, 1984.

attempting a comeback in non-League football with Barnet in 1978, scoring 25 goals from midfield and being named the club's player of the season. After overcoming a battle with alcohol Jimmy turned to television and developed a partnership with Ian St John on a number of shows as well as being a regular columnist in the newspapers and writing a number of books. As successful as he has been in print, nothing matches his successes on the field – 366 goals in 530 appearances for his four clubs is little short of remarkable.

RUUD**GULLIT**

The cream of the crop of Dutch players who emerged in the 1980s, Ruud Gullit was the player who held the national side together, prompting their attacks from midfield and weighing in with some vital goals of his own. Skilful, quick and incredibly strong, Ruud was acknowledged as a versatile player and an asset both in defence and in attack and, at his peak, perhaps the best midfield player in the world.

Born in Amsterdam in 1962, Ruud began his professional career with Haarlem in 1979 and scored 32 goals in 91 games, a more than adequate return for a midfield player. He collected his first cap for Holland whilst at Haarlem too, prompting much speculation that he might be on his way to one of the bigger clubs in the not too distant future.

He eventually moved to Feyenoord in 1982, eventually slotting in alongside Johan Cruyff and helping them win the double of League championship and FA Cup in 1984. Despite this success he moved on the following year to join rivals PSV Eindhoven and was inspirational as PSV won back to back League titles in 1986 and 1987.

Almost as soon as he had his 1987 championship medal in his pocket Italian giants AC Milan swooped and paid a then record fee of £6.5 million to reunite Ruud with his fellow countrymen Marco van Basten and Frank Rijkaard. As well as the three Dutchmen, this great AC side, assembled at great cost by president Silvio Berlusconi, also boasted the talents of Paolo Maldini and Franco Baresi and the result was that AC Milan swept all before them on both the domestic and European front, winning the Serie A in 1988 and with it entry into the European Cup the following season. Ruud, Marco and the rest duly delivered the greatest club prize in club football, winning the European Cup in 1989 and 1990, as well as securing further Serie A titles in 1992 and 1993.

There was no doubt who the star of the show was during this spell, for Ruud was crowned European Footballer of the Year in 1987 and won the World accolade in 1987 and 1989. Ruud also helped AC Milan win the European Super Cup and World Club Championship in 1990, when he was probably at the peak of his career.

Born: Surinam, 1st September 1962

Debut: Holland v Switzerland, 1/9/1981

Appearances: 66 caps for Holland

Honours: League Champion (Holland – 1984, 1986, 1987, Italy – 1988, 1992, 1993), Dutch FA Cup winner (1984), Italian FA Cup winner (1994), Dutch Player of the Year (1986, 1987), European Cup winner (1989, 1990), European Player of the Year (1987), World Player of the Year (1987, 1989), European Championship winner (1988)

Current Status: Retired

Ruud was subsequently appointed manager of Newcastle United in place of Kenny Dalglish and, with a brand of play he called 'sexy football', took Newcastle to the final of the FA Cup in 1999. Despite his constant chewing on his lucky medallion, Newcastle were beaten relatively easily by a Manchester United side pursuing a treble. The following season began disastrously, with Ruud dropping local hero Alan Shearer and having an equally public fallout with his captain Robert Lee and after just five games into the season, following a defeat by local rivals Sunderland, he resigned. According to popular opinion, he resigned before the club could sack him although there is no hard evidence to confirm this.

Since his exit from St James' Park Ruud has done occasional work for British television, usually commenting on European Champions League matches for Sky and playing Sunday football in his native Amsterdam. Still fit enough to play at lower level in the professional game, Ruud claims he cannot face the prospect of three training sessions a week and listening to the same boring pre-match team talks as the reason why he has not pursued his career further! His only direct involvement with the game came with a brief spell in charge of former club Feyenoord during the 2004-05 season, although he left at the end of the season having failed to win the club any silverware. Whether he returns to the game he graced as a player remains to be seen.

Ruud was also able to convert this club form into international success, captaining the Dutch side to victory in the 1988 European Championships, heading home one of the goals in the 2-0 victory over the Soviet Union in the final. This was the first major trophy won by the Dutch, something that had eluded even the likes of Cruyff and Neeskens in their heyday.

Injuries had begun to slow him down a little by the time AC Milan won the title in 1993 and Ruud was allowed to move on to Sampdoria that summer, helping them win the Italian FA Cup in 1994.

A year later he was released on a free transfer and snapped up by Chelsea, where player-manager Glenn Hoddle was assembling a side of all talents. When Hoddle accepted the position of England manager in 1996, Ruud was appointed player-manager of Chelsea in his place.

In 1997 he guided the club to victory in the FA Cup final, becoming both the youngest and the first overseas manager to have lifted the famous trophy. It was the club's first trophy triumph in 26 years and signalled a rebirth for a club that had spent too long in the doldrums. The following season saw Chelsea battling at the top of the table, lying in second place and making progress on all fronts in cup competitions when Ruud was sensationally sacked, the club claiming that there had been a disagreement over pay.

THIERRY**HENRY**

Born: Les Ulis, 17th August 1977

Debut: France v South Africa, 11/10/1997

Appearances: 91 caps for France

Honours: Premier League Champions (2002, 2004), FA Cup winner (2002, 2003, 2005), World Cup winner (1998), European Championship winner (2000), FWA Footballer of the Year (2003, 2004, 2006) – the first player to win this award 3 times, PFA Player of the Year (2003, 2004)

Current Status: Still playing

Arsenal's all-time top goalscorer, it took Thierry Henry just six and a half years to accumulate the 151 League goals he needed to overtake Cliff Bastin, a feat achieved on 1 February 2006 against West Ham. Four months earlier, against Sparta Prague Thierry had overtaken Ian Wright's record in all competitions for the Gunners, netting his 186th goal for the club.

Born near Paris in 1977 Thierry attended the French Football Federation academy at Clairefontaine and played youth football for Les Ulis, Palaiseau, Viry-Chatillon and FC Versailles. His professional career, however, began with AS Monaco where Arsene Wenger was manager and he made his first team debut at the age of 17. Thierry was initially used as a wide player, ostensibly because Monaco already had the talents of Brazilian Sonny Anderson playing down the middle. Eventually Thierry made the striker's berth his own and broke into the French national side, making his debut in October 1997, just in time to break into the squad for the World Cup finals being held in France the following year. Although still not a regular starter, Thierry did come on to change things somewhat in the semi-final against Croatia and to ensure France made it to the final against Brazil, as well as netting three goals during the course of the competition.

His participation in the World Cup did not go unnoticed elsewhere and in January 1999 Juventus paid £14 million to take him to Turin. However, whilst they may have known of his goalscoring abilities they did not make the best of them, pushing him wide out on the wing from where he struggled to make an impact. He scored just three goals in twelve first team appearances before pronouncing himself unable to settle in Italy. Arsene Wenger rescued him from his nightmare, paying £10.5 million in August 1999 to reunite with the player at Arsenal.

In the seven seasons to date, Arsenal have not finished any lower than fourth in the Premiership, winning the title twice. In the same period they have won the FA Cup three times, and Thierry's value to the club can be gauged by the fact that he has been top goalscorer every single season. Whilst he has been known to drift out wide and then cut in towards the middle with a lightning burst of pace, it is as a central striker that he has proved to be most effective, resulting in a plethora of silverware in the Highbury boardroom and the player quickly overtaking Cliff Bastin and Ian Wright in the goalscoring stakes.

Thierry has transferred this goalscoring prowess to the international stage, helping France add the European Championship in 2000 to the World Cup won two years previously, again scoring three goals. In 2003 he

BELOW
Thierry Henry of Arsenal shoots past Kostas Chalkias of Portsmouth to score during their game in 2005.

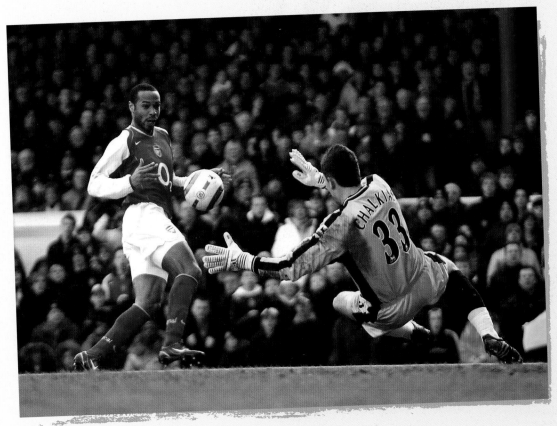

was top goalscorer and named player of the tournament as France hosted and won the Confederations Cup.

Whilst Thierry is vital as a goalscorer to both club and country, there is more to his game than just scoring goals. He has the ability to set up his team mates when they are in a better position than he to score and set up a Premiership record of 20 goals during the 2002-03 season. It is this all round contribution that has earned him accolades and awards from around the world, finishing runner-up in the 2003 and 2004 FIFA World Player of the Year award whilst being named Player of the Year for 2003 and 2004 by both the Football Writers Association and Professional Footballers Association. He has also won the European Golden Boot award, which is presented to the top goalscorer across Europe's major Leagues, in 2004 and 2005, sharing the honour in the latter year with Diego Forlan. Virtually all of his goals are spectacular efforts, as you might expect from a player who is equally gifted with either foot.

At the start of the 2005-06 season Thierry was appointed club captain at Arsenal, replacing the Juventus-bound Patrick Vieira. This, perhaps more than any other accolade, speaks volume for Thierry Henry, for it is very rare in the modern game to have a striker as captain, but Thierry's awareness of what is happening in all areas of the field made him the ideal candidate. The added responsibility has inspired Thierry to some of the finest form of his career, guiding the club through what turned out to be a disappointing season on the domestic front but with potential success in Europe. At the same

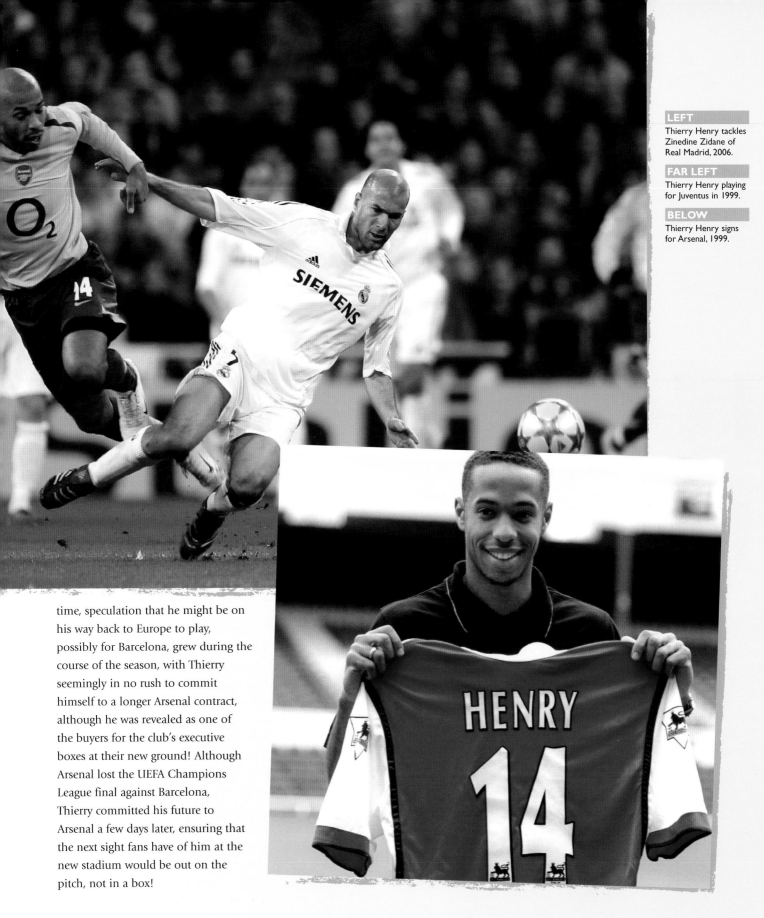

LEFT
Thierry Henry tackles
Zinedine Zidane of
Real Madrid, 2006.

FAR LEFT
Thierry Henry playing
for Juventus in 1999.

BELOW
Thierry Henry signs
for Arsenal, 1999.

time, speculation that he might be on his way back to Europe to play, possibly for Barcelona, grew during the course of the season, with Thierry seemingly in no rush to commit himself to a longer Arsenal contract, although he was revealed as one of the buyers for the club's executive boxes at their new ground! Although Arsenal lost the UEFA Champions League final against Barcelona, Thierry committed his future to Arsenal a few days later, ensuring that the next sight fans have of him at the new stadium would be out on the pitch, not in a box!

NANDOR**HIDEGKUTI**

Virtually all of the media attention directed towards the so-called Magnificent Magyars, the all-conquering Hungarian national side of the 1950s, has tended to focus on Ferenc Puskas and, to a lesser extent, his inside forward partner Sandor Kocsis. The attention they have garnered has tended to overshadow the contribution made by others from that side – the flying winger Zoltan Czibor, the midfield general that was Jozsef Bozsik and the dynamic goalkeeping of Gyula Grosics, and more importantly, the man who made the whole team tick – Nandor Hidegkuti.

Football in the late 1940s and early 1950s was a straightforward sport – the number two shirt was worn by the right back, and he tended to patrol little further than the halfway line since he was primarily concerned with defensive duties. Similarly, the number five shirt went to the centre half, usually the tallest man on the field, who also seldom ventured into the opponents' half as he was also employed to keep the opposition from scoring. And so it ran through the team, with the number nine shirt being worn by the centre forward, a player (at least as far as the British game was concerned) who was able to run through brick walls and take the ball, goalkeeper and anything else into the goal in pursuit of scoring.

And then along came Nandor Hidegkuti. He wore the number nine shirt, but his game did not rely on brawn but brains. To begin with, he did not push forward as far as his two inside forwards, rather he sat back a little, waiting to see if the centre half would follow him out, as he was programmed to do, and so create space for others to exploit. For the plan, which became known as the deep lying centre forward, to work, it needed a player with exceptional ability, speed and accuracy in passing – that man was undoubtedly Nandor Hidegkuti.

Born in March 1922, much of his football development was lost to the Second World War and when the Hungarian side were becoming a major force he was already the wrong side of 30. He had begun his professional career with Second Division side Herminamezo and earned his first cap for Hungary whilst with the club, being called in to replace Ferenc Szusza in an international against Romania. Few outside his own club had heard of Nandor, but after the match, which Hungary won 7-2 with Nandor netting two of the goals, they could talk of little else. Despite this promising start he could not claim to be a regular in the side for another seven years, making only sporadic appearances.

Born: 3rd March, 1922
Died: 14th February 2002
Debut: Hungary v Romania, 30/9/1945
Appearances: 69 caps for Hungary
Honours: Olympic football champion (1952), Hungarian champions (1951, 1953, 1958)
Current Status: Deceased

LEFT
Nandor Hidegkuti scores his team's second goal in the semi-final match against Uruguay during the 1954 World Cup.

BELOW
Nandor Hidegkuti (2nd right) kicks the ball past German goalkeeper Heiner Kwiatkowski as Hungary beat Germany 8-3 during the 1954 World Cup.

He made the squad for the 1952 Olympics in Helsinki (his switch to the army side MTK of Budapest had ensured that 'officially' he was a soldier) and helped Hungary to the gold medal, after which he was first choice at centre forward, replacing his own team-mate Peter Palotas. This was also when he began playing deeper, thus setting in motion countless Hungarian attacks that so bewildered their opponents. This was perfectly demonstrated in the two matches against England in 1953 and 1954 – the meeting at Wembley in 1953 saw England lose 6-3 (Nandor grabbed a hat-trick), the first time they had lost at home. During the course of the match Nandor had baffled three English defenders; Harry Johnston, Billy Wright and Jimmy Dickenson, all of whom had spells trying to mark him out of the game, to no avail. A few months later it got worse for England, beaten 7-1 in Budapest and handed a lesson they never forgot.

Much has been made of the Hungarian record between 1950 and 1955 – played 51, won 43, drew seven lost one, scoring 220 goals and conceding only 58. Unfortunately, the one defeat came in the World Cup final of 1954 against West Germany, a side Hungary had already beaten during the course of the competition! Nandor had one further crack at winning the World Cup, appearing in the 1958 competition even though he was 36 years of age, not quite as fast as he used to be and other countries had come up with their own ways of blunting his effectiveness.

He did, however, manage to help MTK win three League titles during his time with the club, even though he had originally been due to sign for rivals Ferencvaros – according to legend, he overheard two Ferencvaros supporters complaining about an unknown they were about to sign and walked away to link up with MTK.

Whilst Ferenc Puskas and a number of other stars of the Magnificent Magyars side defected following the Hungarian Revolt of 1956, Nandor remained and continued adding to his tally of international appearances until his retirement in 1958. He then turned to coaching, at home and eventually abroad, taking Fiorentina to the European Cup Winners' Cup in 1961 and then returning to Hungary to steer Gyor to the championship. Nandor later coached in Poland and Egypt, being particularly revered in the latter. After suffering from heart and lung problems for some time before his death, he passed away in February 2002 at the age of 79.

JAIRZINHO

Born: 25th December 1944
Debut: Brazil v Uruguay, 24/4/1963
Appearances: 81 caps for Brazil
Honours: World Cup winner (1970)
Current Status: Retired

Brazil's victory in the 1970 World Cup has been largely credited to the inspirational performances of Pelé, but it is arguable whether Brazil would have won the trophy had it not been for the goalscoring abilities of Jairzinho, who became the first and still only player to have scored in every match of a World Cup finals competition, netting seven in Brazil's six matches. This feat was made all the more remarkable by the fact that Jairzinho had had to recover from a twice broken right leg, an injury that at one time threatened his entire playing career.

Although Jairzinho was to become an exceptional winger, he began his professional career at Botafogo at the age of fifteen in a more central role. This was largely because of the presence of Garrincha, still something of a permanent fixture for both club and country on the wing. Gradually however Jairzinho began making more and more appearances on the wing, replacing Garrincha when he was injured and then giving him a battle for the position on a more regular basis. Eventually Botafogo and Brazil worked out how to accommodate both players, with Garrincha operating on the right and Jairzinho on the left.

Jairzinho made his Brazilian debut in 1963 against South American rivals Uruguay and made a considerable impact in the so-called Little World Cup tournament held in Brazil the following year that featured Brazil, Portugal, Argentina and England. The real World Cup, to be held in England, was still two years away and Jairzinho was established as a member of the side when the Brazilian squad was announced.

The story of the 1966 World Cup as far as Brazil was concerned was the way Pelé was kicked out of the competition, with Garrincha also being past his best and unable to influence matches the way he had in years gone by. Jairzinho played in all three of Brazil's matches, used as a left winger against Bulgaria and Hungary and switched to the right against Portugal, but it was all to no avail as far as Brazil were concerned, for they slid out of the competition.

By the time the 1970 competition came around, Jairzinho was one of the more experienced players and would turn out to be the major difference between success and failure. Usually selected in a central position alongside Tostao, Jairzinho was one of those forwards who was liable to turn up in almost any position up front and used his previous experience as a winger to good effect. He scored twice against Czechoslovakia, the

JAIRZINHO

only goal of the game against England (where he appeared almost unnoticed on the right hand edge of the area to smash home the winner) and once in the final group match against Rumania. Thereafter both Jairzinho and Brazil hit top form, with Jairzinho scoring against Peru in the 4-2 quarter-final, against Uruguay in the 3-1 win in the semi-finals and then in the 4-1 final victory over Italy. Despite his seven goals, however, Jairzinho finished second behind Gerd Muller in the Golden Boot stakes, but one suspects that a winner's medal in the World Cup final was more than adequate compensation!

Brazil's success in the competition saw several of their players targeted by Europe's top sides and Jairzinho signed for Olympique Marseille soon after the tournament ended, but unable to settle in France he soon returned home to Brazil to sign for Cruzeiro.

Jairzinho was one of only three World Cup winners who was still in the Brazil side by the time the 1974 competition in West Germany kicked off, even if his attacking prowess had been blunted by the passage of time. Both he and Brazil were goalless in their first two matches, with Jairzinho getting off the mark in the 3-0 win over Zaire that ensured Brazilian progress into the next stage. Jairzinho was to score one more World Cup goal, in the 2-1 win over Argentina, but Brazilian involvement in the competition came to an end after three second-round group matches. By the time the next World Cup came around, Jairzinho was no longer involved on a regular basis, although he won his last cap

for Brazil when in his 38th year, appearing against Czechoslovakia in March 1982, the game being drawn 1-1.

After finishing his playing career in Venezuela with Portuguesa he turned to coaching and would eventually become national coach to the Gabon side, being sacked from the post after Gabon had been knocked out of the 2006 World Cup by Angola. His greatest achievement as a coach, however, came whilst he was coaching Sao Cristovao, spotting a then 14-year-old Ronaldo and recommending him to his former side Cruzeiro. Ronaldo's abilities in front of goal no doubt reminded Jairzinho of a former Brazilian great – himself.

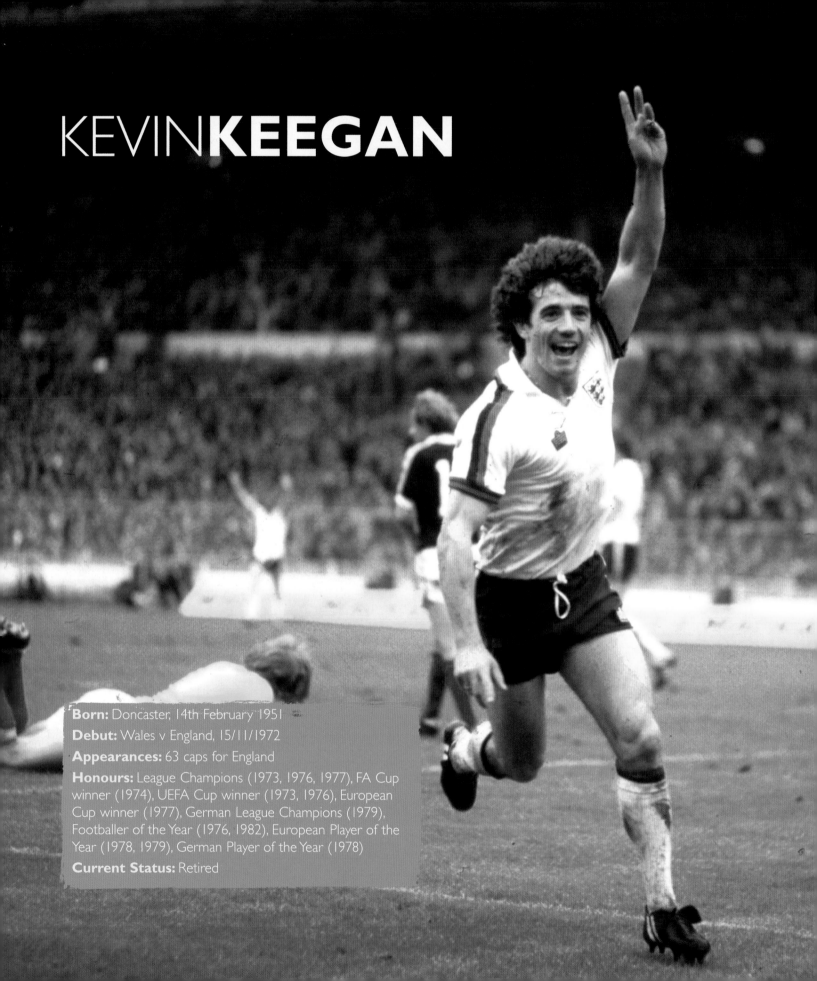

KEVIN**KEEGAN**

Born: Doncaster, 14th February 1951

Debut: Wales v England, 15/11/1972

Appearances: 63 caps for England

Honours: League Champions (1973, 1976, 1977), FA Cup winner (1974), UEFA Cup winner (1973, 1976), European Cup winner (1977), German League Champions (1979), Footballer of the Year (1976, 1982), European Player of the Year (1978, 1979), German Player of the Year (1978)

Current Status: Retired

Kevin Keegan may not have been the most naturally gifted player but his achievements certainly made him one of the hardest working and an inspiration to those around him. It was a trait he was to take into management, his natural enthusiasm overcoming any tactical shortcomings.

Born in Doncaster Kevin joined Scunthorpe United as an apprentice from school and was upgraded to the professional ranks in December 1968. Kevin would go on to make 120 full League appearances for the lowly club, netting 18 goals, not a great return for a player who was invariably played as a forward, but his hard-working runs in midfield did not go unnoticed by the array of scouts that gathered at The Old Showground to plot his progress. Eventually Liverpool manager Bill Shankly stepped in with a £33,000 offer for the player in May 1971 and took him to Anfield.

His progress at Liverpool was little short of phenomenal, for a little over a year later he had collected the first of his five caps for England at Under 23 level and broke into the full side for the European Championship qualifier against Wales. Once he got into the side, there wasn't much that could dislodge him.

He won a host of honours whilst at Anfield, including three League Championships, the UEFA Cup twice, the FA Cup once and, in what turned out to be his Liverpool swan-song, the European Cup in 1977. That summer he was surprisingly sold to SV Hamburg for £500,000

but continued to enhance his reputation on the continent, being named European Player of the Year in both 1978 and 1979 as well as German Player of the Year in 1978.

He helped Hamburg win the Bundesliga in 1979 and the following season was instrumental in getting the side to the final of the European Cup but there was no second winners' medal as Nottingham Forest shut out the threat of Kevin Keegan and managed a 1-0 win.

Although there was considerable speculation that he might end his German career for a return to Liverpool, it was Southampton who surprisingly stepped in during July 1980 and paid £400,000 to take him to The Dell. Although there was to be no repeat of the honours he had won at Liverpool and Hamburg, he was still considered an exciting draw whenever Southampton rolled into town. His international career had continued unabated and by the time the 1982 World Cup came around Kevin had 62 caps to his name. Although he was

widely expected to be one of the first players manager Ron Greenwood put on his team sheet, he was suffering from an injury as the team set off for Spain and undergoing around the clock treatment.

The side reached the second stage without Kevin (or Trevor Brooking, who was similarly injured) and then played out a 0-0 draw with West Germany in the first match of the second stage. They therefore needed to beat host nation Spain by two clear goals in order to qualify for the semi-finals and midway through the second half, with the goals not coming, Ron Greenwood threw on the patently unfit Kevin and Trevor in an attempt to try and rescue the match. In the event neither substitution worked, for had either player been fully fit the chances that fell to them might have been scored and it turned out to be the final appearances for the national side for the pair of them.

Kevin had barely returned from his brief World Cup duty (the only occasion he appeared in the World Cup finals) when he was sold to Newcastle United for £100,000. Although Newcastle were struggling to get out of the Second Division, the challenge of doing so appealed to Kevin and he was made captain, eventually guiding them into the First Division at the end of the 1983-84 season. Kevin promptly retired from playing at the end of the promotion season, reckoning that at 33 he was too old to go chasing around in the First Division. Instead he retired to Spain in order to work on his golf handicap!

He was tempted back into the game in 1992 as manager of Newcastle United and had the same impact

play-offs and set them on the road to reaching
the Premiership.

By the time they got there, Kevin had already gone,
the eventual replacement for Glenn Hoddle as England
manager, initially on a part-time basis but later full time.
He got the side to the European Championships in
2000 after a play-off against Scotland but after a defeat
in the opening game of the 2002 World Cup qualifiers,
at home to Germany in the last match played at
Wembley before the old stadium was torn down, he
announced his immediate resignation.

Kevin returned to the game as manager of
Manchester City and got them back into the Premiership
before retiring towards the end of the 2004-05 season.
He has said that his involvement with football is
finished, one or two pundits predict he will be lured
back again – only time will tell.

as a manager as he had had eight years earlier as a
player, uniting the club to push for promotion to the
Premier League and thereafter chase for honours.

Although he was felt to be tactically naïve his side
was certainly entertaining to watch and had he put a
little more emphasis on defending they might well have
won the Premiership League title in 1996 instead of
allowing Manchester United to catch them. They
finished runners-up behind the same Champions the
following year but by then Kevin had gone, resigning in
January 1997 as the club was about to float on the stock
market. The official reason given was Kevin's reluctance
to commit himself to a long term contract. He
resurfaced as Director of Football at Fulham,
subsequently taking over as manager during the 1997-98

MARIO**KEMPES**

Born: Belville, 15th July 1954

Debut: Bolivia v Argentina, 23/9/1973

Appearances: 43 caps for Argentina

Honours: Spanish Cup winners (1979), European Cup Winners Cup winners (1980), Argentinean Champions (1982), World Cup winner (1978)

Current Status: Retired

Many of the players in this book earned their status as 'legends' as a result of their exploits over an entire career – Mario Kempes earned his, at least as far as Argentinean fans will be concerned, thanks to four matches! Of course there was more to his career than those four matches, but it was his goalscoring exploits in three of those four that ensured his lasting place in Argentinean folklore.

Born in Belville in Cordoba in 1954 he began his career with Instituto Atletico Central Cordoba in 1971 and spent some three years with the club, making his international breakthrough with Argentina during this time. A member of the squad for the 1974 World Cup in West Germany, Mario appeared in all six of Argentina's matches, either on from the start or introduced as a substitute, but failed to score even one of the nine goals his country scored.

Despite this Mario had proved more than capable of scoring at club level and was moved on to Rosario Central in 1974, hitting 85 goals in 105 appearances for the club over the next two or so years. That form alerted a host of European clubs and he was sold to Valencia in 1976, going on to finish his first season in Spanish football as the leading League scorer with 24 goals. He repeated the feat the following season, hitting 28 goals for his club even if Valencia were still some way adrift of winning any silverware.

Mario was the only European-based player included in Cesar Menotti's Argentina squad for the 1978 World Cup being held in Argentina and was an ever-present in the three opening group matches. Once again Mario was unable to get

onto the scoresheet but Argentina qualified for the next stage, second behind Italy. This placing proved to be the making of both man and country, for based away from the capital of Buenos Aires, Argentina were based in Rosario, seen of Mario's earlier triumphs. He grabbed both goals in the 2-0 win over Poland, went close on a number of occasions in the goalless draw with Brazil and then scored twice in the 6-0 demolition of Peru that confirmed Argentina's place in the final. Mario opened the scoring against Holland after 38 minutes and again in extra time to set the home nation on their way to a 3-1 victory, with his tally of six goals in the competition enough to earn him the Golden Boot award.

Expectation rose after this success and Mario proved he was the man for the occasion, helping Valencia win

BELOW
Kempes before the
World Cup in 1982.

the Spanish Cup in 1979 and the European Cup Winners' Cup the following year, even if the European success was achieved in a penalty shoot out after a goalless 120 minutes against Arsenal.

In 1981 Mario returned home to spend a season with River Plate, helping them win the Argentinean Championship at the end of his only season.

The following summer he returned to Spain, initially to try and help Argentina retain the World Cup. The holders reached the second stage before being eliminated, Mario again drawing a blank in his five appearances, which effectively brought a halt to his international career after 43 appearances, during which he had scored twenty goals.

Mario remained in Spain after the tournament, rejoining Valencia, where he had previously earned the nickname The Matador. His second spell was not as successful as his first however, Valencia failing to win any further silverware.

His Valencia contract came to an end in the summer of 1984 and he had a number of trials with other clubs, including a short spell with Spurs, before joining the Hercules club of Spain for two years. Mario's career then took in a succession of minor clubs, including First Vienna, VSE Sankt Polten, Kremser, Fernandez Vial and Pelita Jaya before he finally retired in 1996.

Whilst it was the four matches in the 1978 World Cup that established his reputation, every club he played for and all his opponents would confirm there was a lot more to Mario's game than he was seemingly given credit for. He was extremely hard working and aware of the team ethic, setting up almost as many chances for team mates as he put away himself (Argentina's third goal in the 1978 final was scored by Daniel Bertoni from a Mario Kempes pass).

More importantly, his style of play made it difficult to defend against, for he tended to begin his attacks from outside the penalty area, using his strength and speed to get past defenders and into danger areas, with defenders often not knowing whether they should move out to pick him up early or sit and wait for him to come to them. By the time they made up their minds it was usually too late – he hit 146 goals for Valencia in his 247 appearances, an exceptional strike rate.

JURGEN**KLINSMANN**

It takes a lot to make the gentlemen of the British press change their minds or eat their words. Prior to the sensational events of 29th July 1994, the German striker the rest of Europe knew as 'The Golden Bomber' was derided as 'The German Dive Bomber' in Britain, a reference to Jurgen Klinsmann's tendency to fall over, especially inside the penalty area, at the slightest of touches.

At the press conference to announce his signing by Spurs, he disarmed the media by politely asking for directions to the nearest diving school. A few weeks later, on his League debut, he celebrated his goal by diving across the pitch in celebration. The British press were on his side from there on in.

The son of a baker, Jurgen was born in Goppingen in 1964 and first started playing football at the age of eight, turning out in every available position during his youth, including that of goalkeeper. It was as a striker,

however, that he excelled and at the age of seventeen he was snapped up by Stuttgart Kickers, then in the Second Division of the West German League. Just in case he did not make it as a professional footballer, Jurgen trained under his father and is a qualified baker himself and has been known to help out at the family baker's business on his numerous visits home!

His exploits in the second tier soon had the bigger fish of the Bundesliga circling and he was signed by VfB Stuttgart in 1984 having finished the previous season as top goalscorer in the Second Division. Although he was unable to win the League with Stuttgart (indeed, Jurgen did not help any of his club sides win the League until he was finishing his career with Bayern Munich!) he did help them reach the final of the UEFA Cup in 1989, something of a swansong at Stuttgart for during the summer he was sold to Inter Milan.

Jurgen's arrival at the San Siro was intended to galvanise the Inter side into regular contenders for the title, but whilst he was widely acknowledged as one of the finest finishers in the game, the supply lines from his Inter colleagues were regularly cut off and he struggled to get the goals that would keep Inter at the top end of the table.

The same could not be said at international level. Having made his debut for West Germany in 1987 and appeared in the 1988 European Championships in his homeland, Jurgen journeyed to the 1990 World Cup finals in Italy full of confidence, for with the likes of Rudi Voller and Lothar Matthaus in the side, chances were always likely to be created. The Germans were impressive in the group stages, overcame their stiffest opposition England in the semi-final and got their revenge against Argentina in the final with a 1-0 win, the only goal coming from the penalty spot. Many Italians got a clearer idea of what Jurgen Klinsmann was capable of during the competition, for five of West Germany's matches were played in Milan.

A year after collecting a World Cup winners' medal there was at last silverware at club level, with Inter

Born: Goppingen, 30th July 1964

Debut: Brazil v West Germany, 12/12/1987

Appearances: 108 caps for West Germany/Germany

Honours: World Cup winner (1990), European Championship winner (1996), UEFA Cup winner (1991, 1996), German Champion (1997), Germany Player of the Year (1988, 1994), Football Writers' Association Player of the Year (1995)

Current Status: Retired

Legends of **FOOTBALL**

beating Italian rivals AS Roman 2-1 on aggregate in the UEFA Cup final. This was to be the only trophy win during his spell in Italy, for in 1992 he moved on to join AS Monaco, then managed by Arsene Wenger. Jurgen spent two years in the principality but was in and out of the side, invariably finding himself on the bench and brought on late to try and rescue games if Monaco were behind.

After Germany's unsuccessful attempt to retain the World Cup in America in 1994, Jurgen had made up his mind to leave Monaco. Although there were offers from a number of top Spanish clubs, he opted for the move that would present the greatest challenge and joined Tottenham Hotspur. It was a move that stunned the entire football world – only one German player (Bert Trautmann) had ever enjoyed what could be called a successful career in England whilst Spurs were still reeling from a series of FA imposed punishments, including a twelve-point deduction for the coming season and banned from the FA Cup. Added to this was the club's close links to the Jewish community, which made the signing of a German player even more astonishing and Jurgen's own reputation, which the media were quick to pick up on. Club chairman Alan Sugar won his battles with the FA off the field whilst Jurgen won over a new army of admirers with his performances on it. So much so that when manager Ossie Ardiles was sacked midway through the season, Jurgen was invited to become player-manager, although he turned the offer down in order to concentrate on playing.

His only full season at White Hart Lane ended with the club just short of qualifying for Europe and whilst he had originally signed a two-year contract, he opted to join Bayern Munich during the summer, a move that angered Alan Sugar even though he had agreed to the clause in the contract in the first place. Having helped

Bayern win the UEFA Cup in 1996 he returned to England that summer and was part of the German side that won the European Championships, beating England in the semi-final, again on penalties, along the way.

The following season he finally got to win a League championship medal, helping Bayern win the Bundesliga, and then returned to Italy to play for Sampdoria. The move was not a success, for he found himself confined to the bench once again and, with the World Cup in France looming on the horizon, was in need of regular first team football. Quite by chance Spurs were struggling at the wrong end of the Premiership and a loan deal for the rest of the season was quickly arranged, Alan Sugar having obviously forgiven the German star. Just as he had done previously Jurgen turned the club's fortunes around, scoring four of the goals against Wimbledon that ensured safety in the League.

Jurgen announced his retirement from professional football immediately after the World Cup, another unsuccessful campaign for the Germans, and moved to America in order to take up a position in commercial business. In July 2004 the man who said he'd never go into football management agreed to become the new head coach of the German national side, helping prepare his side for the 2006 World Cup being held in Germany. His decision to remain living in America, coupled with the German side's disastrous form in the run up to the tournament, had many calling for his head before Germany kicked off against Costa Rica. The Germans ultimately exceeded expectations by finishing third, with Jurgen announcing he was to step down immediately after the competition, despite calls for him to remain. There are rumours linking him to the vacant American job, perhaps the ideal position for someone wishing to continue his American residence.

DENIS**LAW**

Like Jimmy Greaves, a goalscorer of equal repute, Denis Law missed the biggest match of his life, despite playing a key role in getting the team to the final. In Denis's case it was the 1968 European Cup final, which Manchester United won by beating Benfica, but Denis had been sidelined by injury since the semi-final stage and thus missed out on United's big night.

Born in Aberdeen in 1940 Denis was addicted to football from a young age, turning down a place at a grammar school since this would have required him to play rugby! Having been presented with his first pair of football boots from a neighbour, Denis showed exceptional abilities as a schoolboy, especially when switched from full back to inside forward and was subsequently selected for Scotland Schoolboys.

He was eventually spotted by Huddersfield Town's Scottish scout and sent to Leeds Road for a trial where the manager remarked 'The boy's a freak. Never did I see a less likely football prospect – weak, puny and bespectacled.' Despite his physical appearance, Huddersfield felt he showed enough promise to sign him in 1955 and arranged for an operation to cure his squint, a squint that had previously meant he'd had to play with one eye closed!

Denis made his debut in December 1956 at the age of sixteen and earned rave reviews almost immediately, prompting Matt Busby to offer £100,000 for him there and then, which was duly turned down. Denis made his international debut two years later and scored in the match against Wales, further adding to his growing reputation. When Bill Shankly, manager of Huddersfield between 1957 and 1959, left for Liverpool he wanted to take Denis with him but Liverpool were unable to raise sufficient funds for his transfer.

In March 1960 he did move on, joining Manchester City for a then record fee of £55,000, although Denis was not particularly keen on the move, since City had narrowly avoided relegation the previous season and Huddersfield were seen as the better side. Denis's time at City was not without its highs and lows, with the player scoring six times in an FA Cup tie against Luton Town before the match was abandoned with twenty minutes to go. In the replayed game, Denis scored again but City lost 3-1 to exit the cup!

In the summer of 1961 he joined Jimmy Greaves in Italy, signing for Torino, although Inter Milan tried to block the move, claiming he had signed a pre-contract deal with them. Just like Jimmy Greaves, Denis Law found life in Italy stifling, with Torino insisting on a clause in his contract that gave them the final say on whether he could be released for international matches.

After surviving a car crash in February 1962 with fellow British team-mate Joe Baker, Denis put in a transfer request in April. Although this was turned down, Denis effectively walked out on the club and was

Born: Aberdeen, 24th February 1940
Debut: Scotland v Wales, 19/10/1958
Appearances: 55 caps for Scotland
Honours: English League champions (1965, 1967), FA Cup winner (1963), European Footballer of the Year (1964)
Current Status: Retired

LEFT
Law scoring during
a game against
Fulham, 1964.

BELOW
Dennis Law in 1960.

Whatever his problems off the field, Denis made a considerable impact on it, helping United win the League title in 1965 and 1967 and picking up the European Footballer of the Year award in 1965. The following season he suffered a recurrence of an old knee injury and was forced to have an operation, although the injury was to cause him problems for the rest of his career. It was enough to keep him out of United's European Cup winning side in 1968, but Denis said that helping Scotland beat World Champions England at Wembley in 1967 was more than adequate compensation!

United reached the semi-final of the same competition a year later, with Denis having a seemingly good goal disallowed as United slipped out. Sir Matt Busby retired at the end of the season and Denis missed most of the following campaign with his knee injury flaring up again. His injury woes continued into the 1972-73 season, with Frank O'Farrell eventually being replaced as United manager by the man Denis recommended, Tommy Docherty. Docherty eventually gave Denis a free transfer in 1973 and the player moved back across the city to re-sign for Manchester City. He played in City's League Cup final defeat that season but is perhaps best remembered for his goal in City's last game of the season, back heeling the ball into the Manchester United net! He believed it was the goal that sent United down (they would have been relegated regardless) and walked off the pitch almost immediately. It was to be his last club appearance, although he did play for Scotland in the World Cup that summer. Upon being told by City manager Tony Book that he was likely to be a reserve team player, Denis duly retired after the World Cup. He went on to work for a number of radio and television stations as a football summariser.

told he would be sold to Manchester United, then Juventus. Denis made it plain he had no interest in joining any other Italian club by returning home to Scotland, reasoning that Torino would rather have Manchester United's money than none, since he had no intention of playing for Juventus. In July 1962 therefore he was sold for another record fee, £115,000 taking him to Old Trafford.

Denis moved in with exactly the same landlady he had boarded with whilst at City and found many other things almost exactly the same at United as they had across the city – United were erratic in the League, struggling to avoid relegation, but fortunately found their form in the FA Cup, a competition they were ultimately to win by beating Leicester City 3-1 at Wembley. That same season saw Denis play in a match that he believed made him a marked man for the rest of his career as far as referees were concerned – after the match against West Bromwich Albion in December 1962, Denis complained that he had been goaded throughout by the referee, and both the player and his manager Matt Busby made an official complaint to the Football Association. A disciplinary committee upheld the complaint and announced that the referee would be severely censured, but he would not accept the censure and quit the game. Denis remains convinced that he was singled out for extra attention from both referees and the game's rulers thereafter.

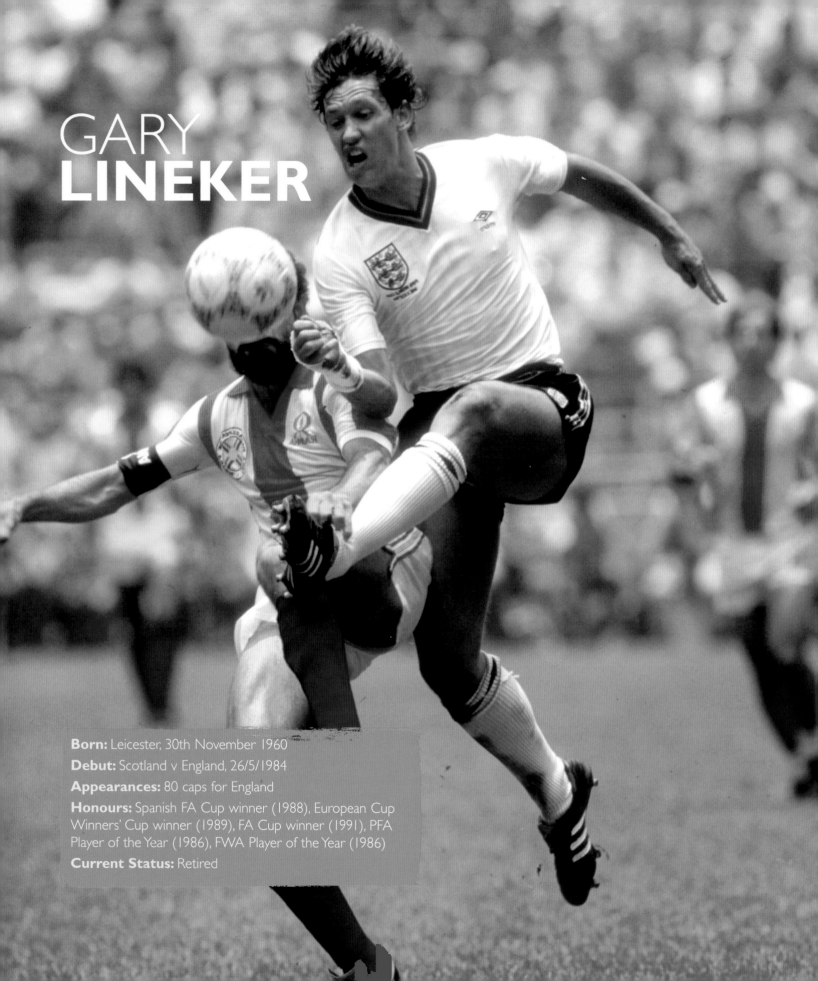

GARY
LINEKER

Born: Leicester, 30th November 1960

Debut: Scotland v England, 26/5/1984

Appearances: 80 caps for England

Honours: Spanish FA Cup winner (1988), European Cup Winners' Cup winner (1989), FA Cup winner (1991), PFA Player of the Year (1986), FWA Player of the Year (1986)

Current Status: Retired

Gary Lineker became known as something of a gentleman footballer, managing to go through his entire career without being so much as booked. As far as some were concerned, this showed a lack of total commitment, overlooking the fact that Gary's real abilities lay inside the opponents penalty area, not picking up yellow cards on the halfway line.

Born in Leicester Gary joined the local club as an apprentice and was upgraded to the professional ranks in November 1979. In and out of the side during his first couple of seasons, Gary began to make a major impact in 1981-82, helping the club to the FA Cup semi-finals and was top goalscorer with 17 goals in 39 League appearances. Over the next three years he hit at least twenty in each season, helping the club back into the top flight and earning growing calls for his call up into the full England side, a call that finally came in May 1984 against Scotland.

Although Spurs were known to have tried to sign him during the summer of 1984, Gary remained a Leicester City player until July 1985 when he joined Everton in a move fixed by a tribunal at £800,000, even though Leicester City had been holding out for £1 million. Gary was in blistering form during 1985-86, scoring thirty goals for the reigning League Champions and helping them to the FA Cup final. Unfortunately, their rivals across the Stanley Park, Liverpool, pipped them at the post in both the League and cup, although personal compensation for Gary was received when he was named Player of the Year by both the PFA and Football Writers Association in 1986.

It was the World Cup in Mexico that summer that made his reputation on a worldwide basis. A hat-trick in the final group match against Poland, a match that England had to win, earned him plaudits from the English media, but his two goals against Paraguay and then one against Argentina alerted the rest of the world to his capabilities. England may not have progressed beyond the quarter-final, but Gary Lineker had done enough to win the Golden Boot award with six goals.

The flight back to Britain had barely landed when Barcelona stepped in with a £2.75 million offer to take him to Spain. He settled in almost immediately at the club and, although they were unable to topple Real Madrid from the top of the League, eventually did enough to win the Spanish Cup in 1988. By then Terry Venables, the manager who had signed Gary, had left and been replaced by Johan Cruyff. Whilst Gary had been first choice striker under Venables, he had to settle for more of a bit part under Cruyff, often being played out on the wing, hardly the ideal place from

which to score goals but Gary was just happy to be playing. In 1989 he played, albeit still out on the wing, in the Barcelona side that won the European Cup Winners' Cup, beating Sampdoria 2-0 in the final.

In July 1989 he was reunited with Terry Venables, the then Spurs manager paying £1 million to take him to White Hart Lane, where he was expected to link up with fellow England internationals Paul Gascoigne and Chris Waddle. Waddle headed off for Marseille and France soon after Gary arrived, but Gary and Paul did forge an exceptional understanding, with Gary getting on to the end of numerous chances Paul created during their first season together.

The following summer saw the World Cup come around again and Gary was to score a further four goals for his country, including two from the penalty spot against Cameroon that took England into the semi-final against West Germany. A typical Lineker strike in that match, bringing England level as time began to slip away earned England extra time, but the Germans won a nail biting penalty shoot out to advance to the final.

Despite the disappointment on a national stage, Gary and Paul were fired up for the 1990-91 season, taking Spurs to the FA Cup final against a backdrop of financial problems that sparked rumours Spurs were desperately trying to sell both key players even on the eve of the final. Whilst Paul Gascoigne had proved to be the inspiration behind Spurs' charge for the final, Gary Lineker's contribution was no less vital, including two goals in the semi-final against Arsenal.

The final itself will not be remembered with any real affection inside the Lineker household, for Gary had a perfectly good goal disallowed and then missed a penalty, but Spurs did come from behind to win the trophy, Gary's first and subsequently only major domestic honour in the game. He was to spend one further season at Spurs, helping the club reach the quarter-finals of the European Cup Winners' Cup and

LEFT
Lineker shoots for Everton during the FA Cup of 1986.

FAR LEFT
Gary Lineker in action for Spurs, 1989.

BELOW
Lineker celebrates after winning the European Cup Winners' Cup for Barcelona in 1989.

semi-finals of the League Cup, albeit without the contributions of an injured Paul Gascoigne.

Gary left Spurs at the end of the 1991-92 and a month later made his final appearance for England, being taken off in the 2-1 defeat against Sweden in the European Championships. He had won a total of 80 caps for his country, scoring 48 goals, an agonising single strike behind England record holder Bobby Charlton. Gary should have at least equalled the record, missing a penalty against Brazil in one of the warm up matches prior to the European Championships.

After a spell playing in Japan Gary returned home to pursue a career in television, subsequently becoming the host to the BBC flagship programme Match of the Day. Here he displays a laid back persona almost in complete contrast to the effort he would expend inside an opponent's penalty area.

JOSEFSEPP**MAIER**

It has always been claimed that England had a knack of constantly turning up world class goalkeepers, especially when one thinks of the likes of Gordon Banks, Peter Shilton and Ray Clemence. The West Germans, as they were then, have also been extremely well served over the years, particularly when one considers the likes of Hans Tilkowski and his eventual replacement Sepp Maier.

Born in Metten in 1944 Sepp, who was born Josef and also acquired the nickname Die Katz (The Cat), in deference to his agility between the posts, spent his entire professional career with Bayern Munich, first

joining the club in 1960 and spending some nineteen years as first choice goalkeeper. To the club he is little short of a legend, revered as much as Franz Beckenbauer and Gerd Muller. Whilst Muller, as goalscorer, and Beckenbauer as captain grabbed most of the plaudits, much of Bayern's success in the 1960s and 1970s owed much to Sepp Maier in goal.

Not only was he difficult to beat, he was almost impossible to dislodge from the Bayern goal, making a record 422 consecutive appearances between 1966 and 1977, a figure that is certainly a German record and may well top the list around the world. His performances for Bayern at club level, helping them win the German Cup in 1966 earned him a call up to the West German squad for the 1966 World Cup in England, making his debut in a warm up match against Ireland in Dublin. However, it was Tilkowski who held the position during the competition, although Sepp's day would come.

Bayern Munich were unrivalled in the domestic game for the next decade, winning the German League four times, the European Cup three times in succession, the European Cup Winners' Cup once and a further three German Cups. Sepp Maier was the last line of defence for all of them, and what a last line in one match, where Bayern were at home and so on top of the game there was little for Sepp to do, he amused himself and half the crowd by chasing a duck that had wandered onto the field of play! The normally reliable Sepp, who had had little trouble wrapping his giant hands around a fast moving football, proved totally unable to catch the duck, despite frequent dives at it! Despite this sometimes flippant approach, Sepp was the model of consistency, a trait that was recognised by him being

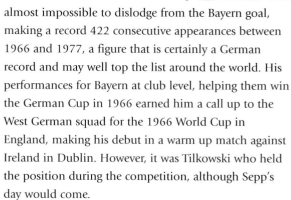

Born: Metten, 28th February 1944

Debut: Ireland v West Germany, 4/5/1966

Appearances: 95 caps for West Germany

Honours: German champions (1969, 1972, 1973, 1974), German Cup winners (1966, 1967, 1969, 1971), European Cup Winners' Cup winners (1967), European Cup winners (1974, 1975, 1976), World Club Cup winners (1976), European Championship winner (1972), World Cup winner (1974), West German Player of the Year (1975, 1977, 1978)

Current Status: Retired

Legends of **FOOTBALL**

Bayern were German champions and European champions as well.

The West Germans so nearly retained the European Championship in 1976, only losing to Czechoslovakia in a penalty shoot out after the final had finished all square at 2-2. By the time the next World Cup came around, in 1978 in Argentina, Sepp's better days were already behind him and although he performed admirably, he could do little to prevent the side going no further than the second round. He continued as goalkeeper for the national side until 1979, having collected an impressive 95 caps in the process.

Whether his career could have lasted longer is open to some debate, but a serious car accident, in which he suffered injuries that were initially seen as life-threatening, brought his career to a halt. He eventually recovered and turned to coaching, remaining at Bayern Munich where he is still goalkeeping coach. He also assisted the national squad but was relieved of his position in October 2004 after offering his opinion as to whom coach Jurgen Klinsmann should select   Bayern goalkeeper Oliver Kahn, with whom Sepp worked with every day, or Jans Lehmann of Arsenal!

LEFT
Maier catches the ball in front of Johan Cruyff as Franz Beckenbauer looks on during the World Cup final, 1974.

BELOW
Sepp Maier in action during the 1978 World Cup.

named German Player of the Year three times, a remarkable accomplishment for a goalkeeper, even more so when one considers the team-mates who were ahead of him on the park at Bayern.

By the time the 1970 World Cup came around, Sepp was first choice goalkeeper for West Germany and helped them reach the semi-final, where they were beaten by Italy 4-3 and also missed out on appearing in the third and fourth place play-off. Two years later Sepp played a significant part in helping the Germans lift some serious silverware as the European Championship was won in something of a canter, beating the Russians 3-0 in the final. This proved to be merely the first course in a fine meal, for two years later the Germans won the World Cup, coming from behind to beat Holland 2-1. This was probably the peak of German domination of the game World champions, European champions and

DIEGO**MARADONA**

Born: Lanus, Buenos Aires, 30th October 1960

Debut: Argentina v Hungary, 27/2/1977

Appearances: 91 caps for Argentina

Honours: Argentinean Champions (1981), Italian
Champions (1987, 1990), Italian Cup winners (1987), UEFA
Cup winners (1989), World Cup winner (1986), Argentinean
Player of the Year (1979, 1980, 1981, 1986), South American
Player of the Year (1979, 1986, 1989, 1990, 1992), European
Player of the Year (1986), World Player of the Year (1986)

Current Status: Retired

At his best he was virtually unrivalled as the most exciting player in the world, able to change games in an instant. Unfortunately, there was another, darker side to Maradona, one which saw him press the self-destruct button on more than one occasion.

Diego displayed such abilities as a youngster he made his League debut for Argentinos Juniors ten days before his sixteenth birthday and went on to make eleven appearances for the side during the remainder of the season. In February the following year he became the youngest player to earn international honours for Argentina, making his debut in the 4-1 victory over Hungary. Such was Diego's development, he was widely considered to be a certainty for the Argentina World Cup squad for 1978, a tournament that Argentina was hosting.

Manager Luis Cesar Menotti became concerned that Diego was being pushed too early and decided to omit him from the squad, a decision that could have proved disastrous if Argentina failed to win the competition, but a 3-1 extra time victory over Holland vindicated Menotti and seemingly allowed Maradona to continue his march to his own destiny.

Named South American Player of the Year in 1979 and 1980, Diego scored 116 goals in 166 League appearances for Argentinos Juniors before being sold to Boca Juniors for £1 million. Two years later Argentina began the defence of their world title, having effectively rebuilt the 1978 side around the mercurial talents of Diego Maradona.

Whether it was eagerness to make up for the personal disappointment of 1978 or the weight of expectation placed upon him, the 1982 tournament was not one that Diego would care to remember with much affection. He scored two goals in the opening round of matches, which ensured Argentina progressed into the next group stage, but two defeats, against Italy and Brazil and a dismissal for retaliation in the Brazil match spelt the end of Argentina's reign as World Champions and a disappointing tournament on a personal basis for Diego Maradona.

Diego remained in Spain after the World Cup, having been sold to Barcelona (where Cesar Luis Menotti was manager) for nearly £5 million, then a world record fee for a player. His time with the Catalan club was not a success, suffering a bout of hepatitis which robbed him of some three months of his career and meant he made only 36 League matches in two years. Indeed, so disappointing was the move that after two years both club and player were looking for a way

BELOW

Maradona in action for Napoli, in the 1989 UEFA Cup Final.

out and a transfer to Italian club Napoli for £6.9 million was arranged in the summer of 1984. Despite the cost, Napoli recouped almost immediately, selling 40,000 season tickets as soon as Maradona's arrival was announced.

If Napoli had expected Diego to turn their side into League Champions in an instant they were to be disappointed, although the club did improve their League placing, finishing eighth at the end of the first season and third a year later, although Diego suffered a niggling knee injury during that second season, one which at one point threatened his presence in the World Cup squad for Mexico.

Diego recovered sufficiently to take his place in the side and had a hand in all three of his country's goals in their opening match against South Korea. His stature grew with each passing match, propelling Argentina towards the final. It was the quarter-final clash with England that made his reputation on a world-wide basis, netting one goal with barefaced cheek (to put it mildly) and another with sublime skill to establish him as the greatest player in the world. Two goals in the semi-final and an inspirational performance in the final were enough to make Argentina World Champions again.

Maradona continued that form into the domestic season with Napoli, helping them win the double of League and Cup in 1987. Two years later they won the UEFA Cup and the following year, 1990, reclaimed the League title, a fitting close to a season that was to see Argentina once again try and defend their World title, in Italy. Although Diego Maradona inspired his side

FIFA knew exactly what drugs he was taking to control his weight and that they (FIFA) had agreed to overlook the matter if he would appear in the competition, also claiming FIFA reneged on the deal. No one will know for sure if there was such a deal (which seems unlikely), but this signalled a rapid end for Maradona's career and reputation. He later served a fifteen month ban for cocaine use (a drug that has never been prescribed for weight control!) and after leaving Napoli in 1992 wound down what had at times been a wondrous career with Seville, Newell's Old Boys and his former club Boca Juniors.

Like many of his peers, Maradona found it extremely difficult to make the transition from player to coach and spells working with Mandiyu and Racing Club promised much but delivered little. He virtually severed all ties with the game he once graced in 1997.

LEFT
Maradona holds off Klinsmann of West Germany in the 1990 World Cup.

FAR LEFT
Maradona runs with the ball.

BELOW
Maradona kisses the World Cup trophy, 1986.

through to the final, they were unimpressive virtually the whole way and in the final itself lost self discipline, two players and one goal as they were beaten by West Germany. Diego Maradona had tears flowing down his cheeks as the Germans collected the trophy, but his performances in the competition meant he cried alone.

Four years later Maradona was still an important feature of the Argentina side. Battling to combat a weight problem he made just two appearances in the competition, scoring a typical goal against Greece and then failing a drug test after the Nigeria match and was sent home in disgrace. Maradona was later to claim that

STANLEY MATTHEWS

Stan Matthews spent over thirty-three years as a professional player and had an international career that stretched over twenty two years but is chiefly remembered for his exploits in just one match, the 1953 FA Cup final.

Born in Hanley the third son of a professional boxer (Jack Matthews, the Fighting Barber of Hanley), Stan was a schoolboy star and was capped for England at that level against Wales before signing with Stoke City. Stan was made a professional in February 1932 and within two years had made his first appearance for England, scoring in the 4-0 win over Wales. Stan retained his place for the next match, a 3-2 victory over World Champions Italy, but the game was marred by a string of hard tackles by both sides and became known as the Battle of Highbury. Stan was at his best running with the ball against opponents who wanted to try and tackle him fairly, so he had an anonymous match against the Italians. He was equally quiet on a couple of other occasions, prompting one journalist to write 'I saw Matthews play just as moderately in the recent inter-League match, exhibiting the same slowness and hesitation. Perhaps he lacks the big match temperament.'

The England selectors obviously thought so for a time and he would make only one appearance for his country between November 1934 (the match against Italy) and his eventual recall on a permanent basis in November 1937. That came in the politically charged friendly against Germany at Tottenham, with Stan helping England to a 3-0 victory. When he returned, he made the most of the chance, scoring England's first in the 2-1 win over Wales and a hat-trick in the next match, a thrilling 5-4 win over Czechoslovakia with England down to ten men.

The following year, 1938, he rocked Stoke by requesting a transfer. The news caused a furore in the city, with 3,000 fans holding a protest meeting and more than 1,000 marching on the stadium carrying placards politely asking Stan to reconsider – he withdrew his transfer request and stayed.

With the outbreak of the Second World War Stan enlisted in the Royal Air Force and although he was officially stationed at Blackpool, managed to guest for Crewe Alexandra, Manchester United, Wrexham, Arsenal and Rangers. He also made 29 appearances for the national side in wartime internationals and even made one appearance for a Scottish XI.

Stan returned to Stoke at the end of the hostilities but was soon unsettled, with Stoke eventually selling him to Blackpool for £11,500 in May 1947. Ultimately it was his combination with Stan Mortensen that was to pay dividends for the club, with Blackpool reaching the FA Cup final in 1948, 1951 and 1953. Blackpool had already tasted defeat in 1948 and 1951 and were

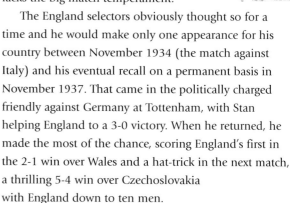

Born: Hanley, 1st February 1915
Died: 23rd February 2000
Debut: Wales v England, 29/9/1934
Appearances: 54 caps for England
Honours: FA Cup winner (1953), Player of the Year (1948, 1963), European Player of the Year (1956)
Current Status: Deceased

Legends of **FOOTBALL**

LEFT
Blackpool's Stanley
Matthews dribbles
past a Bolton player
in 1953.

BELOW
Stanley Matthews
after receiving his CBE
at Buckingham Palace
in 1957.

heading the same way in 1953, for they were 3-1 down with less than twenty minutes to go when Stan Matthews took over. Weaving up and down the right wing, he carved out chance after chance for his forwards, Blackpool eventually winning 4-3 thanks to a Stan Mortensen hat-trick and the winner from Bill Perry. The entire country, with the exception of Bolton inhabitants, had willed Stan Matthews to victory, his only major honour in the game.

Stan had been an England regular immediately after the war and retained his place until 1949 when the selectors chose to utilise the younger legs of Tom Finney. Eventually a way was found to accommodate both wingers, but not before the damage had been done, for Stan made just one appearance during the 1950 World Cup finals, the final group match against Spain when England were all but eliminated.

Stan made two appearances in the following World Cup, having a major impact in the first match against Belgium when he switched to inside forward midway through a match England were trailing in and inspiring a comeback that earned England a point in the 4-4 draw. His final World cup appearance came in the 4-2 quarter-final defeat by Uruguay.

Although Stan helped England during their qualification for the 1958 World Cup, appearing in three matches, all of which were won, he was not part of the squad for the finals in Sweden. Indeed, his international career had already come to an end, his final appearance, nearly twenty-three years after his first, coming in the 4-1 win over Denmark in May 1957 and

with 54 caps to his name. Had the Second World War not intervened, who knows how many caps he could have accumulated in the same period.

Whilst his international career may have finished, Stan had no plans to hang up his boots just yet. In 1962, at the age of 46, he returned to Stoke City and proved the inspiration behind a side that would go on to win the Second Division title and return to the top flight. His final appearance eventually came in February 1965 when he returned to the Stoke side after twelve months out with a knee injury – he was now in his fiftieth year. Astonishingly, Stan always maintained that he retired too early!

Whilst his career may have been somewhat barren as far as medals were concerned, the 1953 Cup final notwithstanding, Stan had been honoured all along the way, being named Player of the Year by the Football Writers' Association in 1948, the first player so honoured. In 1956 he was named European Player of the Year, again the first player to be given the honour. Stan's effect on Stoke upon his return earned him another Player of the Year award in 1963 and two years later, when he retired, he was knighted for his services to football, the first footballing knight.

Stan had a brief spell in management with Port Vale, although it was not a success and so he moved to Malta where he coached (and occasionally played for) Hibernians. He later coached in South Africa and Canada and was still turning out for local sides well into his sixties. His impact on the game was such that when he died, in 2000, more than 100,000 people lined the funeral route in Stoke, all of whom had come to pay their respects to one of the greatest sportsmen of all time.

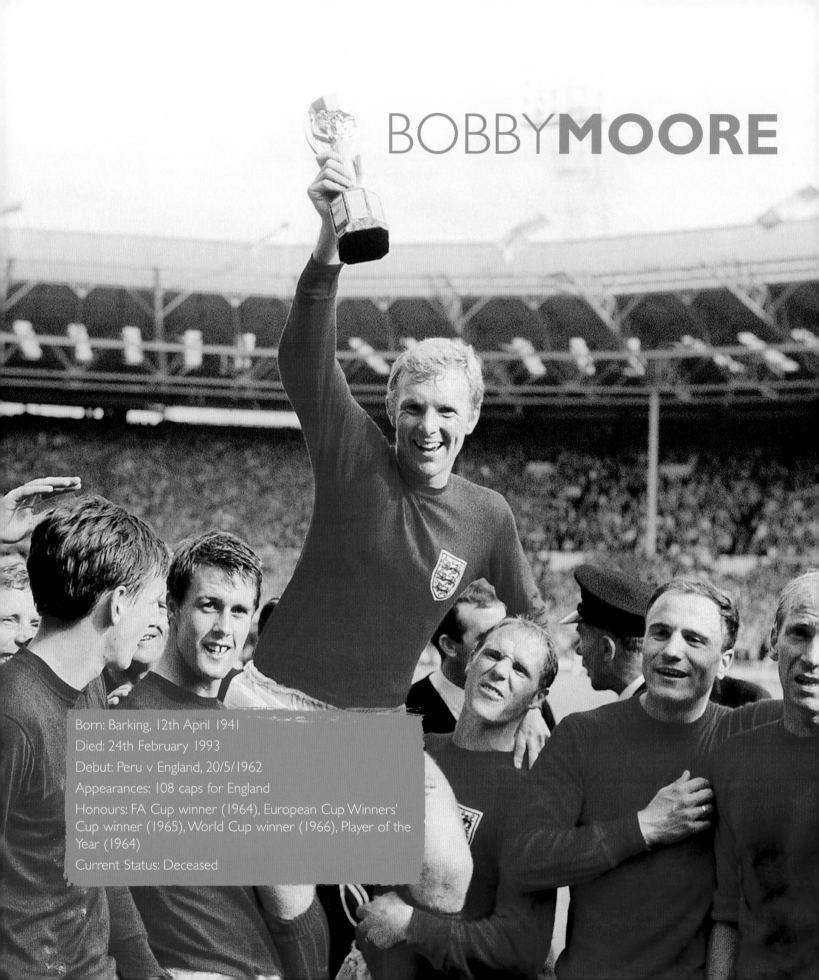

BOBBY**MOORE**

Born: Barking, 12th April 1941

Died: 24th February 1993

Debut: Peru v England, 20/5/1962

Appearances: 108 caps for England

Honours: FA Cup winner (1964), European Cup Winners' Cup winner (1965), World Cup winner (1966), Player of the Year (1964)

Current Status: Deceased

There are a few players whose club allegiances count for little or nothing – their passing is greeted with sadness around the entire country, football fans recognising the contribution that player made on the international scene. Bobby Moore, captain of the side that won the World Cup in 1966, falls into that category, his death from cancer in 1993 being mourned throughout the football world.

Born in Barking in April 1941, Bobby joined West Ham United as a schoolboy and eventually signed professional forms in June 1958. Given a debut in September against Manchester United, he soon established himself as a regular within the side, going on to make 544 League appearances for the Hammers, only one of which was as a substitute.

He made his England debut against Peru in Lima in May 1962, just in time to stake a place for the World Cup squad of that year and emerged at the end of the tournament, which saw England reach the quarter-finals, as one of the few English successes.

Over the next four years, Bobby became acknowledged as one of the best half backs in the domestic game and proved that by helping West Ham to the FA Cup in 1964 and the European Cup Winners' Cup the following year (West Ham just missed out on winning a trophy for a third consecutive year in 1966, finishing runners-up in the League Cup). Both those victories, against Preston North End and TSV Munich 1860 respectively, were achieved at Wembley and ended with Bobby climbing the 39 steps to collect the

trophy. In 1966 he made the same journey to collect the greatest prize in football, the World Cup.

Whilst there were many successes in the England side that year, with Gordon Banks confirming his status as one of the best 'keepers in the world, Geoff Hurst hitting a hat-trick in the final, a feat that has never been equalled, let alone beaten, and the all-action style of Alan Ball also earning plaudits but there was no better performer during the entire competition than Bobby Moore. Alf Ramsey's change of tactics midway through the competition, leaving out wingers, might have exposed Bobby and his fellow half backs, but Bobby had the composure to work out how to nullify the extra danger. Indeed, such was his composure that in the final itself, with England hanging on to a 3-2 lead in the final moments of extra time, he won the ball on the edge of the England penalty area and ignored the shouts of those around him to belt the ball as far away as he could and instead looked for a

BELOW
Bobby Moore in action for Fulham during a Division One match played at Craven Cottage.

measured pass for Geoff Hurst to run onto to eventually complete his hat-trick. Not surprisingly, Bobby was voted the player of the competition.

By the time the next World Cup campaign came around, Bobby's reputation was even greater. It had survived a number of bust-ups with his managers, both domestic and international, for both Ron Greenwood and Alf Ramsey had no doubt that Bobby could produce the goods when it really mattered. Bobby's Mexico campaign did not get off to the best of starts, falsely being accused of stealing a bracelet in Colombia, but if the accusers thought they could ruffle Bobby Moore, they picked on the wrong player. His performances in the competition, especially against eventual Champions Brazil, were of the highest quality – even Pelé acknowledged Bobby Moore as a worthy opponent.

Bobby's international career carried on to 1973, making his 108th and final appearance against Italy in a friendly at Wembley in November 1973. That was less than a month after England had gone out of the 1974 World Cup competition, their inability to beat Poland proving their undoing. Bobby had missed the Poland match, with his replacement Norman Hunter making the mistake that led to Poland's goal in the 1-1 draw. Oh, how England could have done with the composed performance of Bobby Moore that night.

The following year Bobby called time on his West Ham career, moving across London to sign for Fulham for £20,000. There was to be one final appearance at Wembley to savour too, Fulham reaching the FA Cup

Legends of **FOOTBALL**

than spells at non-League Oxford City and then Southend United. For some reason, no one appeared to want to take a chance with Bobby Moore as a manager, a dreadful loss to the game. Instead Bobby moved into journalism, a role that at least enabled him to make regular appearances in the Press Box at his beloved Wembley.

The announcement that Bobby was suffering from cancer came as a shock to the entire world of football, but it was confidently expected that Bobby would treat the threat as calmly as he done any of his opponents. The news, therefore, of his death on 24th February 1993 rocked the whole country and there was a minute's silence held at every ground in the country in his honour.

LEFT
Bobby Moore the captain of West Ham United and England in 1965.

FAR LEFT
A portrait of Bobby Moore.

BELOW
West Ham United captain Bobby Moore lifts the FA Cup in 1964.

final in 1975 where they faced West Ham! The story didn't quite have a fairytale ending, for West Ham were to win 2-0. Bobby then had a brief spell in America with Seattle Sounders (Bobby even played for Team America in an unofficial international against England during his time in the United States) before calling time on his playing career, although he was lured out of retirement in 1982 to play alongside Pelé, Ossie Ardiles, John Wark, Sylvester Stallone and Michael Caine in the film Escape To Victory.

Whilst Bobby was widely expected to go into management or coaching, his career extended no further

GERD**MÜLLER**

One of the most prolific goalscorers of all time, Gerd Müller's exploits in front of goal earned him the moniker Der Bomber and the record of having scored more goals in World Cup finals than any other player.

Born in the small village of Zinsen, where there was no football pitch, Gerd had to make a seven mile bus journey in order to have a trial with TSV Nordlingen. The death of his father whilst Gerd was still relatively young prompted the youngster to leave school and become apprenticed as a weaver, but he successfully came through his trial with TSV Nordlingen (even wearing borrowed boots!) and was offered a contract with the club.

Despite the fact he struggled with his weight, a problem that earned him his first nickname of Dicker (fatty), he still scored 46 goals in two seasons for the club, prompting interest from Bayern Munich (Müller was signed on the recommendation of President Wilhelm Neudecker, even though coach Tchik Cajkovski was unimpressed). His move to Bayern got off to a poor start, breaking his arm in a reserve team match. He eventually recovered and made it a scoring debut for the first team, going on to net 35 goals that helped Bayern earn promotion into the Bundesliga.

Gerd managed to get the better of his weight problems, with his leaner look making him even quicker off the mark. He grabbed 28 goals during the 1966-67 season, enough to make him joint top goalscorer in the League, and made his West German debut the same season. It was his goals that enabled Bayern Munich to become trophy hunters, collecting the German Cup in 1966 and 1967, also winning the European Cup Winners' Cup in 1967.

As sweet as this success was, it was the domestic League and qualification into the European Cup that interested Bayern most, and after a couple of seasons of near misses, they finally grabbed the title in 1969. After winning the Cup in 1971, there were three League titles in succession to savour, being crowned Champions in 1972, 1973 and 1974.

It was this particular Bayern Munich side that entered folklore, for with Franz Beckenbauer marshalling things at the back and Gerd Müller's goals up front, the Germans had a side that could challenge for the greatest of all club prizes, the European Cup. Bayern managed to win the trophy three times in succession too, winning in 1974, 1975 and 1976.

Born: Zinsen, 11th November 1945

Debut: Turkey v West Germany, 12/10/1966

Appearances: 62 caps for West Germany

Honours: German Champions (1969, 1972, 1973, 1974), German Cup winners (1966, 1967, 1969, 1971), European Cup winners (1974, 1975, 1976), European Cup Winners' Cup winners (1967), European Champions (1972), World Cup winner (1974), German Player of the Year (1967, 1969), European Player of the Year (1970)

Current Status: Retired

Legends of **FOOTBALL**

LEFT
Müller scores for
West Germany during
the World Cup final
in 1974.

BELOW
Müller strikes at the
goal, 1967.

Gerd announced his retirement from international football immediately after the 1974 World Cup win, as good a time as any to leave the international stage. He continued to play on the domestic front with Bayern, as noted earlier, helping them to confirm German superiority in Europe as well as at home.

He remained with Bayern Munich until 1979, having topped the goalscoring charts for the last time in 1978 with 24 goals. In all he was to hit 365 League goals in 427 appearances and had scored more than 600 goals in all competitive matches.

Although he initially expressed a desire to retire completely, he was persuaded to head across the Atlantic and moved to America in 1979 to play in the North American Soccer League, finally retiring from playing in 1982. He later coached at Bayern Munich, trying to instil into Bayern's youngsters the same kind of qualities he had displayed on the field – superb positional sense, immense strength to hold on to the ball when required and speed in twisting and turning out of trouble and into goalscoring opportunities.

As noted earlier, Gerd had made his national debut during the 1966-67 season, appearing in the first match the West Germans played after their World Cup defeat in England, although he was unable to score in the 2-0 win against Turkey. He was omitted from the side until the following April, getting on the score sheet four times in the 6-0 win over Albania.

Gerd was not a regular in the West German side until 1969 but broke into the side at pretty much the right time, being named in the squad for the World Cup finals in Mexico. He was to prove his worth in Mexico, netting ten goals to finish the tournament's top goalscorer as the Germans finished third.

Four years later, with the finals being held in Germany, Gerd scored a rather more modest four goals, but they did include the winning goal in the final against Holland. Gerd's fourteen goals in World Cup finals enabled him to haul himself ahead of Juste Fontaine, who scored 13 in the 1958 competition.

Gerd had also been an integral part of the side that had won the European Championship in 1972, netting two of the goals in the 3-0 final win over the USSR. In all Gerd was to score 68 goals for West Germany in just 62 appearances, conclusive proof that he was virtually without equal as a goalscorer.

JOHAN**NEESKENS**

Whilst Johan Cruyff was afforded most of the accolades during the 1970s as both Ajax at club and Holland at international level demonstrated the concept of 'Total Football', the contribution made by his team-mate Johan Neeskens should never be underestimated. He may have been known as 'Johan the Second', but Neeskens didn't play second fiddle to anyone.

Born in Heemstede in 1951, Johan began his career with the local RCH Heemstede club in 1968 and was quickly spotted by the burgeoning Ajax club and transferred to Amsterdam in 1969. There he linked up with Johan Cruyff and together the two helped turn Ajax into the most exciting club in the whole of Europe. The pair were the lynchpins and powerhouses of a midfield (although Neeskens was originally used as a full back) that propelled Ajax to three consecutive European Cup triumphs, in 1971, 1972 and 1973, adding the World Club championship in 1972 (Ajax declined to take part in either 1971 or 1973, having observed the sometimes volatile nature of the fixtures) and the European Super Cup in 1973 and 1974.

Whilst Neeskens' background as a more defensive-minded midfield player meant he was not a regular on the scoresheet, unlike his namesake Cruyff, he did weigh in with a number of vital strikes. Nowhere was this more evident than on the international stage. First capped by Holland in 1970, Neeskens was one of the key players that guided Holland to the World Cup final in 1974 and finished top goalscorer for the Dutch, netting five goals. One of these came in the final itself against West Germany, a penalty after just two minutes after Johan Cruyff had been brought down before any German player had even touched the ball. Johan Neeskens had developed a particularly effective format for taking penalties: since he believed the goalkeeper would make up his mind early about which way to dive, Neeskens would invariably drive the ball straight down the middle!

After the World Cup Neeskens linked up again with Johan Cruyff and former Ajax manager Rinus Michels at Barcelona, hoping to revive the fortunes of a club that had been almost permanently overshadowed by their rivals in Madrid. Although both Johans proved

Born: Heemstede, 15th September 1951

Debut: East Germany v Holland, 11/11/1970

Appearances: 49 caps for Holland

Honours: Dutch champion (1972, 1973), European champion (1971, 1972, 1973), Spanish Cup winner (1978), European Cup Winners' Cup winner (1979), European Super Cup winner (1973, 1974), World Club champion (1972)

Current Status: Retired

had a spell back in America with Fort Lauderdale Sun before winding down his career with FC Baar and FC Zug, finally hanging up his boots shortly before he turned 40 in 1991.

Johan then turned to coaching, eventually becoming assistant coach to the Dutch national side for the 1998 World Cup under Guus Hiddink. Hiddink resigned at the end of the competition and was replaced by Frank Rijkaard, with Johan assisting him in the quest for the European Championship in 2000. Both men left the national side after the competition, with Johan entering club management with NEC Nijmegen and was able to guide them into European competition for the first time in twenty years in 2003, although he was sacked the following year after a string of poor results.

In December 2005 he linked up again with Guus Hiddink, this time with the Australian national side, and helped them qualify for the 2006 World Cup and make excellent progress in the competition. With Hiddink already announcing his intention to move on to new pastures once the World Cup was over, the Australian FA had hoped to persuade Johan Neeskens to take over, but Johan subsequently signed a contract to join Barcelona, where he will again work alongside Frank Rijkaard.

extremely popular acquisitions by the club, they were unable to bring much success on the field, with only a Spanish Cup in 1978 and the European Cup Winners' Cup in 1979 being delivered to the Nou Camp.

In 1978 Johan Neeskens journeyed to Argentina for the World Cup with his Dutch team-mates, although Cruyff declined to make the trip (it was believed to have been in protest at the military junta in power in the country, but his actual reasons may have been a little more closer to home). Despite the absence of Cruyff, Holland again made it all the way through to the final, although Johan Neeskens found that it was defensive duties that concentrated his time in this tournament, failing to find the net during a competition in which Holland were destined to finish as runners-up.

In 1979 Johan Neeskens surprisingly left Barcelona to head across the Atlantic to sign for New York Cosmos, the latest in the high-profile purchases the Americans were making in an attempt to popularise football (or soccer) in the country. Despite the reduced quality of football Johan was now playing, he was still capped by Holland, collecting the last of his 49 caps in a World Cup qualifier against France in 1981.

After five years in America Johan returned to Europe and signed for FC Groningen for one season. He then

MICHAEL**OWEN**

Whilst Wayne Rooney may have overtaken him as England's youngest goalscorer, Michael Owen has his sights set on other honours – not since the days of Gary Linker has there been a striker able to mount a serious challenge on Bobby Charlton's record of 49 goals for his country – Michael is still fourteen goals short at the time of writing but, assuming he can steer clear of further serious injury, he stands a good a chance of beating the record and setting a new one for himself.

Although Michael was an Everton fan as a youngster, he was taken on by local rivals Liverpool as a junior and was upgraded to the professional ranks in December 1996. Michael earned representative honours for England at schoolboy and youth level before making his League debut for his club, finally coming off the bench against Wimbledon and scoring what would go on to become a trademark goal; outpacing the defence and slotting the ball coolly past the goalkeeper.

Michael's appearance on the international scene was no less impressive and when he made his debut against Chile in February 1998, he became the youngest player to have turned out for England in the twentieth century, his 18 years and 59 days beating former record holder Duncan Edwards by 124 days.

It was that summer's World Cup finals in France that alerted the rest of the world to his prowess, coming off the bench to score against Romania and then hitting a superb individual effort against Argentina in the second round. Collecting the ball virtually on the halfway line, Michael showed a remarkable turn of pace and great close control to take him passed two defenders and then fire in an angled shot that gave the goalkeeper little or no chance of saving it.

Although defences may have been made aware of Michael's abilities, there still seemed to be no guaranteed way of keeping him quiet throughout an entire match. Like many of his goalscoring predecessors, Michael can do little or nothing for 89 minutes of a match and then pop up in the final moments to grab the winning goal. Nowhere was this highlighted better than Liverpool's record breaking 2000-01 season, especially in the FA Cup final against Arsenal, for although Liverpool were largely outplayed, Michael grabbed both goals with virtually his only touches of the ball during the game. Michael also helped the club win the League and UEFA Cup during the same season, but it was Liverpool's inability to mount a serious title challenge that led to speculation that he could be lured away from the club.

Although he helped Liverpool win the League Cup again in 2003, he would not commit his long term

Born: Chester, 14th December 1979
Debut: England v Chile, 11/2/1998
Appearances: 80 caps for England
Honours: FA Cup winner (2001), League Cup winner (2001, 2003), UEFA Cup winner (2001)
Current Status: Still playing

that was likely to become even worse after Real Madrid signed a couple of new strikers, proved the catalyst for his desire for a move away. Although he was known to favour a move back to Anfield, Liverpool's refusal to meet Real Madrid's valuation of £17 million (which would lead to a profit of some £9 million) made that move a non-starter. Although there was a late bid from schoolboy favourites Everton, Michael eventually signed for Newcastle United on transfer deadline day in August 2005.

Whilst Michael had broken into the Liverpool first team on a regular basis owing to Robbie Fowler's long term injury, he has himself suffered a number of strains and pulls that have left him sidelined for lengthy spells. The worst of these occurred on New Year's Eve in 2005, when he broke a couple of bones in his foot during the match against Spurs. When it was later revealed that the pins had been incorrectly set, it became likely that Michael had played his last League match for the season. Michael was faced with a race against time to get himself fit in time for the World Cup in June, although he was encouraged by Eriksson's admission that he would take him to Germany even if not fully fit. When Michael did eventually play in the tournament he was yet again injured and played no further part in the competition.

future to the club, preferring to see whether the club could build a side capable of challenging for the League title and make a serious attempt to win the European Champions League. Similar claims were made regarding Steven Gerrard, but with his contract having longer to run, the desire for Liverpool to cash in on his worth was not as great as it was in Michael's case. There he began the 2004-05 season sitting on the bench as Liverpool kicked off their Champions League campaign, thus ensuring he was not cup-tied for any potential buyers. Real Madrid eventually landed him for a cut-price £8 million, a low fee but still more than Liverpool would have received if he had been allowed to walk out of the club on a free transfer at the end of the season.

He did not enjoy the best of times at Real Madrid, spending more time warming the bench than he did playing on the field, but he still managed to score more than his fair share of goals. What made his situation all the more frustrating was that despite his goals Barcelona still won the Spanish Championship, well ahead of Real Madrid, and to rub salt in the wounds Liverpool ended up winning the Champions League after one of the greatest comebacks of all time.

Although still a regular in the England side, his lack of regular first team football at club level, a situation

DANIEL PASSARELLA

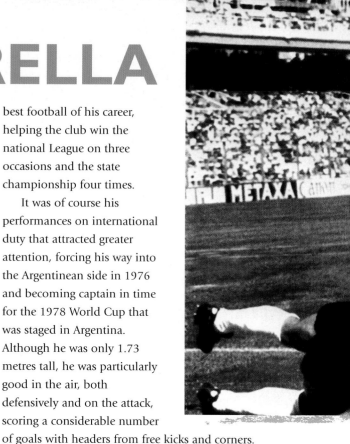

Captain of the Argentinean side that won the World Cup in 1978, Daniel Passarella was a stylish and commanding sweeper in the side, ostensibly employed to prevent the opposition from scoring. However, Daniel could also be relied upon to venture further upfield and scored a highly impressive 22 goals in his 70 appearances for his country, a tally even a striker would be happy with.

Born in the Buenos Aires suburb of Chacabuco he began his career with Sarmiento of Junin before switching to the River Plate club. There he played the best football of his career, helping the club win the national League on three occasions and the state championship four times.

It was of course his performances on international duty that attracted greater attention, forcing his way into the Argentinean side in 1976 and becoming captain in time for the 1978 World Cup that was staged in Argentina. Although he was only 1.73 metres tall, he was particularly good in the air, both defensively and on the attack, scoring a considerable number of goals with headers from free kicks and corners.

Although the weight of expectation hung heavily on Argentina during the competition, Daniel Passarella and his team-mates responded to the challenge. Their final second-group stage match against Peru required a 4-0 win in order to progress to the final; Argentina won 6-0 with Daniel scoring the final goal that ensured a place in the final against Holland. It was Daniel that led the Argentina protests over the bandage on Rene Van der Kerkhof, a move that was seen at the time as little more than gamesmanship but which was probably more inspired by sheer hunger for victory, searching for anything that might unsettle the Dutch and make the Argentinean job that much easier. Although the Dutch forced extra time, Daniel and the rest of the Argentina side were not to be denied their place in history and extra time goals from Mario Kempes and Daniel Bertoni ensured a 3-1 victory. It was Daniel Passarella who thus became the first Argentinean to get his hands on the World Cup, an honour he deserved after his all-action displays during the tournament.

Whilst a number of team-mates headed to Europe in search of financial gain after the World Cup, Daniel remained loyal to River Plate. He was still a regular in the national side that went to Spain to defend their title

Born: Chacabuco, 25th May 1953
Debut: Soviet Union v Argentina, 20/3/1976
Appearances: 70 caps for Argentina
Honours: World Cup winner (1978, 1986), Argentinean Metropolitanos champions (1975, 1977, 1979, 1981), Argentinean National champions (1975, 1979, 1981)
Current Status: Retired

experiences as a player, Daniel continually courted controversy by refusing to select any player who had, in his opinion, excessively long hair or earrings and also stated he would not select any homosexuals! If Argentina had won the World Cup in 1998 he could have selected or omitted anyone he liked, but a quarter-final elimination at the hands of Holland brought his time in charge to an end.

He then turned up as coach of bitter rivals Uruguay with a brief to take them to the finals of the 2002 competition in Japan and South Korea. Uruguay eventually achieved qualification, but they did so without Daniel Passarella, who left his post during qualification in protest at the problems getting Uruguayan players released for international duty.

Daniel then returned to club management, taking over at Parma in Italy, CF Monterrey (he took them to the Mexican championship in 2003) and Corinthians before finally returning home to take over at River Plate once again in January 2006.

in the 1982 World Cup and was one of the few successes in a side that went out at the quarter-final stage. He was still in the squad for 1986 in Mexico, although a bout of enterocolitis meant he did not make a single appearance during the tournament, his place being taken by Jose Luis Brown. Daniel was also reported to be less than enamoured with the relationship between coach Carlos Bilardo and replacement captain Diego Maradona, claiming that both had conspired to keep Daniel out of the side. Whether it was true or not, it fashioned Daniel Passarella's own management style in later years.

At club level Daniel had remained a River Plate player until 1982 when he had finally joined the trail to Europe, signing for Fiorentina and spending four years with the Florence club before switching to Inter Milan for a further two seasons. At the end of his successful spell in Italy Daniel returned to River Plate where he finally finished his playing career in 1989. In all he had made 298 appearances in the Argentinean League (scoring 99 goals, then a record for a defender) and 152 appearances in Serie A (scoring 35 goals).

Daniel then turned to coaching, taking over at River Plate and guiding them to a number of League titles before taking over as national coach in time for the 1998 World Cup in France. Remembering his own

PELÉ

Born: Tres Coracoes, 23rd October 1940

Debut: Brazil v Argentina, 7/7/1957

Appearances: 92 caps for Brazil

Honours: Sao Paulo State Champion (1956, 1958, 1960, 1961, 1962, 1964, 1966, 1967, 1968), World Club Champions (1962, 1963), World Cup winner (1958, 1962, 1970), South American Player of the Year 1973

Current Status: Retired

There have been many contenders and even pretenders to the throne, but Pelé is still untouched as the greatest player to ever grace the game. There has yet to be an opinion poll, whether taken amongst the media, the fans or players that has failed to put Pelé at the very top of the list, the only place he deserves to be. A sign of his influence is that the two factions in the Nigerian Civil War in 1970 agreed to a 48 hour cease-fire so that they could watch Pelé play in an exhibition match in Lagos!

Born in Tres Coracoes the son of Fluminense player Joao Ramos do Nascimento, also known as Dondinho, it was not a foregone conclusion that Pelé (he was given the nickname whilst at school and hated it!) would follow a career as a professional player, for his mother was concerned that he would be like his father and not make a decent living at it. Fortunately, Pelé's talent was obvious at a young age and he was scouted by Waldemar de Brito and after a spell with Clube Atletico Bauru taken to Santos at the age of fifteen. De Brito was so sure of Pelé's future he told the Santos directors they would be signing a player who would become the greatest in the world. Santos offered Pelé professional terms and he responded by scoring four goals on his debut.

Top scorer in the League at the age of sixteen, Pelé did not have long to wait before getting an international call-up and made his debut in 1957, just in time to establish himself in the squad for the World Cup the following year. Expectations were high that Brazil might at last win the greatest competition in the game and Pelé helped his country fulfil their destiny,

even if he arrived in Sweden carrying an injury. He made his first appearance in the final group match against the Russians, hitting the post and laying on one of the goals in the 2-0 victory. He scored the only goal of the quarter-final against Wales, got a hat-trick in the semi-final against France and then netted two in the 5-2 victory over hosts Sweden in the final to finally enable Brazil to get their hands on the trophy. Still only seventeen, Pelé openly wept at the end of the final as the magnitude of what had been achieved began to sink in.

Although there were often rumours of a move to Europe, where there was bigger money to be made, Pelé remained faithful to Santos, preferring to remain in Brazil and help the club to numerous state Championships. That he could have made just as considerable an impact on the European stage was highlighted by Santos' two victories in the World Club Championship, in 1962 and 1963.

PELÉ

Pelé was considered to be even more important to the Brazilian national side and was part of the squad that sought to retain the World Cup in 1962, but after scoring in the 2-0 victory over Mexico he tore a thigh muscle in the second match against Czechoslovakia and was out for the rest of the tournament. Despite his absence, Brazil did go on to win the competition, beating Czechoslovakia in the final.

If there was personal disappointment in 1962, then it was collective disappointment four years later in England. Although Pelé inspired Brazil to win their first match against Bulgaria 2-0, scoring one of the goals from a free kick, it was a laboured Brazilian performance and Pelé had been singled out for some harsh tackling. Pelé was thus missing when Brazil lost their next match against Hungary, their first defeat in the World Cup for twelve years, and there was a sense of desperation when he was brought back, still not perfectly fit, for the final group match against Portugal. The record books show that it was a throw of the dice that went wrong, for Portugal won 3-1 to top the group, but the treatment dished out to Pelé in particular bordered on savagery, with Vicente and Morais the culprits. The tackles were so bad that Pelé was forced off the field for a time, hobbling back on towards the end as Brazil made a vain attempt to keep in the competition.

Such was the experience for Pelé he vowed never to play in the World Cup again, but fortunately was persuaded to change his mind for the 1970 competition. By then Pelé was 29 years old, one of the older and more experienced players alongside talent such as Jairzinho, Rivelino and Tostao, and all would be better protected by referees than Pelé had in 1966. The result was the greatest side in the world winning the World Cup with some of the greatest displays ever witnessed, and Pelé was at the front of all of them. He is best known for three chances with which he didn't score; an outrageous lob from the halfway line against Czechoslovakia after he had spotted the goalkeeper off his line, an equally adventurous dummy on the Uruguayan goalkeeper and a header against England

LEFT
Pelé scores for the Allied POWs during the match against Germany featured in the filming of *"Escape to Victory"*, 1982.

FAR LEFT
Pelé in action for the New York Cosmos, 1970.

BELOW
Pelé celebrates with his team-mates during the World Cup final between Brazil and Italy in 1970.

that had goal written all over it until Gordon Banks dived to tip it over the bar. Pelé did get on the score sheet during the competition, including a powerful header in the final against Italy that set Brazil on the way to a 4-1 victory.

That was Pelé's last appearance on the world stage, for by the time of the next World Cup in West Germany in 1974, Pelé had retired from the international game. He remained a Santos player until retiring at the age of 34 and Santos marked the occasion by retiring his number ten shirt, the inference being that no one could fill it. A year later he was lured out of retirement by the North American League, joining New York Cosmos and later appearing for Team America in the Bicentennial Tournament in his final two years as a player. He would later appear in the film Escape To Victory, going through his entire bag of tricks alongside the likes of Sylvester Stallone and Michael Caine.

Pelé avoided the temptation to become a coach or manager, not least because the man who had relied throughout his career on playing on instinct, backed by his two-footed abilities, couldn't possibly teach lesser mortals the game. Instead he became a sporting ambassador and had a spell as Brazil's Minister of Sport. In more recent times he has been an advocate for children's rights at UNICEF and a figurehead for a charity involved in erectile dysfunction!

Legends of **FOOTBALL**

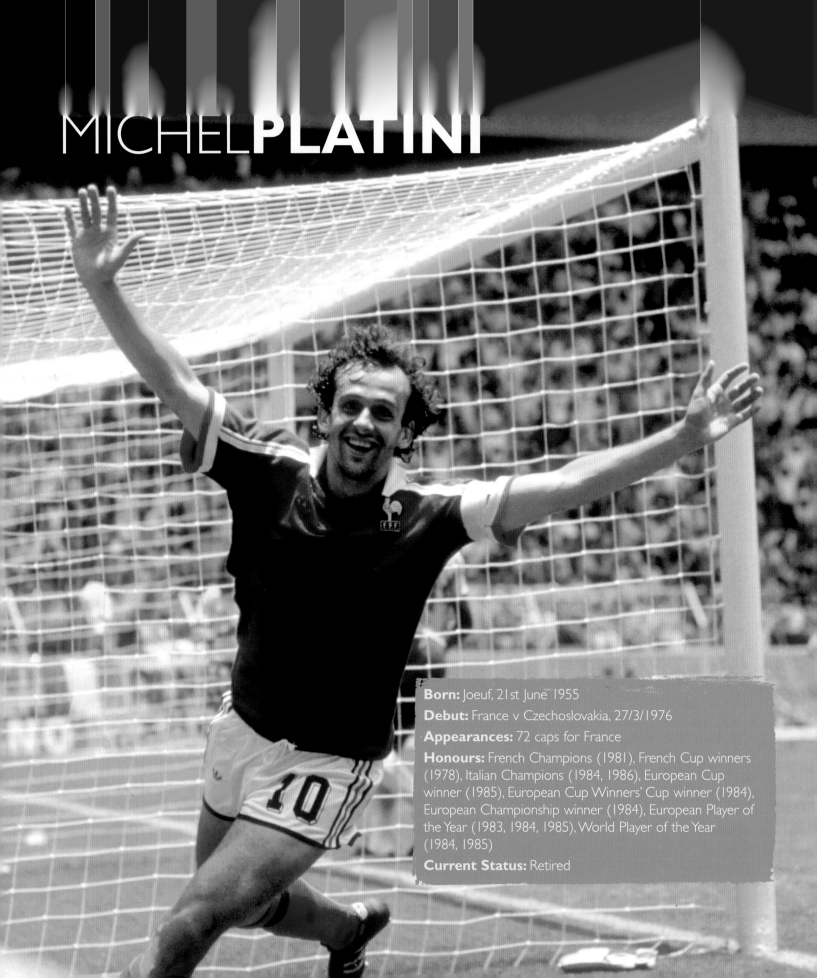

MICHEL**PLATINI**

Born: Joeuf, 21st June 1955

Debut: France v Czechoslovakia, 27/3/1976

Appearances: 72 caps for France

Honours: French Champions (1981), French Cup winners (1978), Italian Champions (1984, 1986), European Cup winner (1985), European Cup Winners' Cup winner (1984), European Championship winner (1984), European Player of the Year (1983, 1984, 1985), World Player of the Year (1984, 1985)

Current Status: Retired

The French have always been known for their fluid, adventurous and attack minded attitude, with today's heroes such as Thierry Henry and Zinedine Zidane continuing that legacy. It was the side of some twenty or so years ago, built around the mercurial talents of Michel Platini that set the benchmark for French football, seemingly for the rest of time.

Born in Joeuf on 21st June 1955 of Italian descent, Michel began his career with Nancy, where his father Aldo was one of the coaches. The Platini's worked hard to fashion Michel's abilities, spending hours working on free kick routines alone, with Michel working on being able to bend the ball around a defensive wall with ease thanks to his practice efforts against a row of dummies set up on the training field.

Michel put those hours of training to good use on the actual field, going on to score 98 goals for Nancy in 175 League appearances and helping them win the French Cup in 1978, scoring the winner against Nice. He appeared for the French in the Olympic Games in Montreal in 1976, the same year he made his full debut for the national side and had become something of a regular by the time the 1978 World Cup in Argentina came around. Although the French started brightly, taking an early lead against Italy in their opening match, they soon faded and were eliminated after the group matches.

Upon returning to France Michel was transferred to St Etienne and would ultimately help the club win the French Championship, netting 21 goals in their 1980-81 Championship season. Michel also scored the bulk of the goals that took St Etienne to consecutive French Cup finals

but this time they both ended in defeat, in 1981 and 1982.

That latter summer saw the World Cup finals in Spain, a tournament where Michel and his fellow countrymen Alain Giresse, Didier Six and Maxime Bossis were widely expected to enhance their reputations on the international stage. They did not disappoint either, for although Michel only netted two goals in the tournament, he was the inspiration behind the French march to fourth place. It might have been even better, for only a disgraceful refereeing decision in the semi-final against West Germany robbed them of a clear cut penalty and the chance to further extend the French lead.

Almost as soon as the competition was over Michel was on his travels, sold to Juventus after scoring 58 goals in 107 League appearances for St Etienne. Although Michel gelled almost immediately with his new team-mates, netting an impressive 16 goals in his first season with the club, turning them into potential

BELOW
Platini in action for Juventus, 1990.

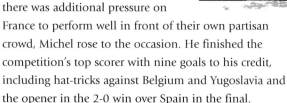

Champions took a little while longer, for Juventus had to be content with finishing second in the League and runners-up in the European Cup. Michel's contribution during the 1982-83 season did not go unnoticed, however, for he was voted European Player of the Year, eventually going on to take the award for three consecutive years.

The 1983-84 season proved to be the most successful of Michel's career, guiding Juventus to the Serie A title and finishing top goalscorer with 20 goals. He also helped Juventus win a double that season as Porto were beaten 2-1 in the final of the European Cup Winners' Cup. That summer saw the European Championships being held in France, and whilst there was additional pressure on France to perform well in front of their own partisan crowd, Michel rose to the occasion. He finished the competition's top scorer with nine goals to his credit, including hat-tricks against Belgium and Yugoslavia and the opener in the 2-0 win over Spain in the final.

Michel would net another winner a year later, scoring from the penalty spot in Juventus' 1-0 win over Liverpool in the European Cup final, but the result was largely forgotten in the aftermath of what became known as the Heysel Stadium disaster and whilst the winners' medal was gratefully received, it was still somewhat tarnished by the deaths of so many Juventus fans.

Michel was to score 12 goals the following season, enough for Juventus to win the Serie A once again, but Michel was thinking of the forthcoming summer long before the season ended, for with the World Cup finals to be held in Mexico, this would surely be his last chance to lift the trophy as a player. Once again he and his countrymen came agonisingly close, finishing in

LEFT

Platini and Belgium goalkeeper Jean Marie Pfaff manage to avoid each other in the European Championships, 1984.

FAR LEFT

Michel Platini of France in action, 1986.

BELOW

Platini proudly holds the European Championship trophy after France beat Spain 2-0, 1984.

third place when it looked as though they might make the final. Indeed, having put out Brazil, albeit on penalties (although the usually reliable Michel was one of the guilty French players who missed) in the quarter-finals, the French could have been forgiven for thinking that they had done the hard part, but once again the Germans did for them in the semi-final, this time without the assistance of the referee.

Michel sat out the third and fourth place play-off against Belgium, thus missing out on an opportunity of adding to his tally of goals at international level. By the time his career came to an end after 72 internationals, he had 41 goals to his name, the new national record. His domestic playing career lasted one further season after Mexico, with Michel ending his career after scoring 68 goals in 147 matches for Juventus, a more than impressive tally. He was just 32 years of age when he hung up his boots, but since he would have been too old for the next World Cup, what was there left for him to play for?

He had already begun to develop a career in television and the media but was eventually persuaded to move into coaching, serving as French national coach between 1988 and 1992. Thereafter his involvement has been in more of a back seat capacity, although he enjoyed a high profile as one of the organising committee for the 1998 World Cup finals held in France. There Zinedine Zidane and his compatriots fulfilled Michel Platini's destiny.

Legends of **FOOTBALL**

FERENC**PUSKÁS**

Dismissed by an English opponent as being too fat shortly before Hungary met England in 1953 and rejected by several Italian clubs several years later for much the same reason, Ferenc Puskás seemed to go through his entire playing career proving his detractors wrong and punishing them where it really hurt, out on the field

Born in Budapest in 1927 he was something of a child prodigy and made his debut for Kispest, his father's old club, at the age of 16. The subsequent occupation by the Soviet Union and the transition of the country to a Communist satellite affected every aspect of life in the country, and football was not immune. The Kispest side were taken over by the authorities and in 1948 became Honved, effectively the Hungarian army side. Technically, all of the players in the team were serving soldiers, although the only thing Ferenc Puskás, given the nickname the Galloping Major ever got to patrol was one touchline or the other!

It did not take Honved long to cement their domination of the domestic game in Hungary, going on to win four League titles during Ferenc's spell with the club. As Ferenc was technically a soldier, he was eligible to play for Hungary in the Olympic Games, being captain as they won the gold medal in 1952 in Helsinki. As rewarding as this success was, the bigger prize was the World Cup, to be held in Switzerland in 1954.

Built around five truly great players in Puskás, goalkeeper Grosics, half back Bozsik and forwards Kocsis and Hidegkuti, with Puskás operating just behind the two forwards, the Hungarians were a formidable team. England found this out to their cost over the space of six months, suffering a 6-3 home defeat (their first defeat at the hands of an overseas nation) in November 1953 and a 7-1 hammering in Budapest the following May. It was not just the scoreline that embarrassed England; it was the manner of the defeats, for in each department the Hungarians were technically superior. Puskás may have been carrying a little bit too much weight, but when you could control the ball as sweetly as he did, the weight didn't matter.

Not surprisingly, the Hungarians were installed as favourites to win the World Cup and made short work of their group opponents Turkey and West Germany, notching up a 17-3 score in their two matches. Ferenc was injured during the match against the Germans and sat it out as Hungary battled to a 4-2 win over Brazil in the quarter-final, although the Brazilians were later to claim that Puskás had attacked and injured a Brazilian player during the course of the match! Ferenc was still out injured for the semi-final, a 4-2 win over the Uruguayans.

Born: Budapest, 2nd April 1927

Died: 17th November 2006

Debut: Hungary v Austria, 19/8/1945

Appearances: 84 caps for Hungary, 4 caps for Spain

Honours: Hungarian Champions (1950, 1952, 1954, 1955), Spanish Champions (1961, 1962, 1963, 1964, 1965), European Cup winners (1959, 1960), World Club Championship (1960), Olympic Champion (1952)

Current Status: Deceased

Legends of **FOOTBALL**

That 7-3 victory over Eintracht Frankfurt saw the great Alfredo Di Stefano score a hat-trick but Ferenc Puskás eclipsed even him, netting the other four. Such was his ability, despite his advancing years, he still managed to net 35 goals in 39 European Cup matches, including another three in a final, although this time, in 1962, Real were beaten by Benfica 5-3.

Hungary had already beaten the West Germans with ease once during the competition and confidently expected they would do so again in the final. Perhaps that was what persuaded Ferenc Puskás to declare himself fit enough to play in the final, even though it soon became apparent that he was plainly struggling. For eight minutes it didn't matter, for Ferenc scored one of the goals that put Hungary on the way to opening a 2-0 lead, but the Germans fought back and six minutes from time took the lead at 3-2. Puskás had the ball in the net before the final whistle blew but the goal was ruled out for offside and the Hungarian and Puskás' gamble had failed.

Honved carried on where they had left off after the World Cup and were competing in the European Cup in Spain when the Hungarian uprising took place in 1956. Puskás, along with Kocsis and Czibor used the uncertainty and confusion to announce they were defecting to the West. Ferenc spent a year in Austria but was unable to get a playing permit and so moved to Italy. There the general consensus was he was too old and too fat to be of any use and various clubs turned him down. Then his old Honved manager Emil Oestreicher came to his rescue, giving Ferenc a £10,000 signing on fee to join him at Real Madrid. It turned out to be one of the best deals Real Madrid ever did.

He was to play an integral part in two European Cup triumphs, in 1959 and 1960, with the latter widely regarded as one of the finest club displays ever seen.

Ferenc became a naturalised Spaniard and appeared for the country in the 1962 World Cup finals in Chile, although Spain finished bottom of their group and Puskás made a minimal contribution. He remained a Real Madrid player until 1966, retiring just before his turned 40 to concentrate on coaching. His success as a coach was limited too, although he did guide the unfancied Panathinaikos to the European Cup final in 1971 where they lost to Ajax.

In 1993 Ferenc Puskás returned home to Hungary, accepting a call to take over as national coach of the side battling to make it to the World Cup finals in America. That particular battle was lost, but for Ferenc Puskás, one of the greatest players Hungary had ever produced, the chance to go back to the country he had defected from four decades previously was proof he had been forgiven. Not only forgiven, but welcomed back with open arms.

RONALDINHO

Born: Porto Alegre, 21st March 1980

Debut: Brazil v Venezuela, 26/6/1999

Appearances: 71 caps for Brazil

Honours: Spanish Champions (2005), World Cup winner (2002), Copa America winners (1999), Confederations Cup winners (2005), European Player of the Year (2005), World Player of the Year (2004, 2005), Champions League winner (2006)

Current Status: Still playing

Brazil keeps producing players of exceptional quality, with every one of them over the last forty or so years being compared to the great Pelé. One or two have been worthy of comparison, including the likes of Zico and Ronaldo, but no one has yet managed to eclipse the original master. Maybe Ronaldinho will be one?

Born in Porto Alegre in the Rio Grande Do Sul region of the country, Ronaldiinho as he is more commonly known (the name is Portuguese for 'Little Ronald', in order to differentiate him from Ronaldo) excelled at futsal and beach football, two variations of the game that enabled Ronaldinho to develop his amazing ball control. Indeed, it was his performances in a number of futsal tournaments that first alerted the world that here was a major star in the making, with numerous clubs paying close attention to his development.

Ronaldinho justified that attention, going on to be top scorer in the World Under 17 Championship in Egypt for Brazil. By then he had been linked with the Gremio club, going on to prove that he was a predatory striker in the regional League in his home country. His exploits at club level eventually led to international recognition, with Ronaldinho scoring the winning goal against Venezuela in 1999 that enabled Brazil to lift the Copa America,

Whilst he remained at Gremio until 2001, there were countless offers from the cream of Europe for Ronaldinho to come to the continent and ply his trade at a much higher level. Whilst he had the pick of the crop, he opted to join Paris Saint-Germain, signing a five-year contract with the French club.

The following year Ronaldinho was part of the Brazilian side that won the World Cup for the fifth time, although he had mixed fortunes during the tournament, scoring an outrageous 35-yard lob over David Seaman in the quarter-final clash with England and later getting sent off for a foul on Danny Mills. That the foul was at best innocuous was confirmed after the match, for although a red card is usually accompanied by a two match ban, which would have ruled Ronaldinho out of the final, it was overturned and he served a one match ban. He was in the starting line-up for the final but substituted by Juninho during the game, one which Ronaldo stamped his authority on.

Whilst there were plenty of team-mates who could assume responsibility within the Brazil side, the same could not be said for Paris Saint-Germain – if Ronaldinho didn't play, or play well, then neither did Paris Saint-Germain. The strain sometimes got to

BELOW

Ronaldinho playing for Barcelona reacts after being tackled by Leonardo Ponzio of Real Zaragoza during a Primera Liga match, 2006.

RONALDINHO

Ronaldinho; his manager Luis Fernandez was to claim that the player was more focused on the Parisian nightlife than on his football, a slur that particularly hurt Ronaldinho. Thus in 2003, when Paris Saint-Germain failed to qualify for European football, Ronaldinho made it known that he would like to move to another club. Having perhaps made a mistake in 2001, he was determined to make amends in 2003.

The bidding soon developed into a two horse race between Spanish giants Barcelona and Premier League champions Manchester United. Both could offer regular European football but in the end Ronaldinho opted for the Catalan capital, joining Barcelona in a deal worth 27 million Euros.

The arrival of Ronaldinho galvanised Barcelona, for they were to finish second in La Liga at the end of his first season at the club, this proving to be the launch pad for a Championship winning season a year later. Whilst Ronaldinho is undoubtedly seen as the brightest star in the galaxy that is Barcelona, he has proved time and time again that it is a collective effort, creating chances for the likes of Samuel Eto'o, Henrik Larsson and Ludovic Giuly as well as scoring more than his own fair share.

Barcelona would be a good side without Ronaldinho; they are a great one with him. His performance in Barcelona's 3-0 win over bitter rivals Real Madrid at the Bernabeu Stadium in November 2005, where he scored two of the goals, earned him a standing ovation from the home crowd – that hadn't been done for any player for more than twenty years.

Whilst Ronaldinho left Paris Saint-Germain for Barcelona in order to participate in European football on a regular basis, thus far Europe has not provided the success that he might have expected, although that could be about to change. It is the consecutive clashes with Chelsea in the UEFA Champions League that are seen as a marker for both Ronaldinho and Barcelona; beaten in the second round on aggregate in 2004-05, Barcelona triumphed a year later and eventually saw off Arsenal in

Legends of **FOOTBALL**

the final, although Ronaldinho did not impose himself on the match as had been expected.

Come the summer and thoughts will again turn to the World Cup, with Ronaldinho now a key member of the side rather than a bit part player. Indeed, he was captain of the Brazilian side that won the Confederations Cup in 2005, proof of his growing importance to his country. His abilities have been recognised the world over, earning him the accolade of World Player of the Year in 2004 and 2005. His exploits in 2006 thus far, guiding Barcelona to victory in the UEFA Champions League and retaining the La Liga title, would appear to make him a leading contender for the title in 2006 – victory in the Champions League and a reasonable performance during the World Cup would merely rubber stamp it.

RONALDO

Born: Bento Ribeiro, 22 September 1976
Debut: : Brazil v Argentina, 23/9/1994
Appearances: 97 caps for Brazil
Honours: : Spanish Champions (2003), Dutch Cup winners (1996), European Cup Winners' Cup winners (1997), UEFA Cup winners (1998), World Cup winner (2002), Copa America winner (1997, 1999), European Player of the Year (1997, 2002), World Player of the Year (1996, 1997, 2002)
Current Status: Still playing

Acknowledged as one of the best strikers in the game, with an amazing turn of pace, dribbling ability and an uncanny knack of being in the right place at the right time have earned Ronaldo the nickname O Fenomeno – The Phenomenon. He has delighted the fans at every club he has played for, but the growing number of clubs has led to criticism that he is something of a football mercenary. He has not manufactured the moves himself, however, and each club he has played for has been extremely well rewarded financially for parting with one of the best strikers in the game.

Born in the Rio de Janeiro suburb of Bento Ribeiro in 1976, Ronaldo grew up playing football in the streets and soon had others singing his praises. It was former Brazilian star Jairzinho who first picked up on Ronaldo's abilities, recommending him to both the Brazilian youth team and his own former club Cruzeiro Esporte Clube, who promptly signed him the very moment he was old enough to enter into a professional contract.

By the time he was 16 Ronaldo had scored 59 goals in just 57 matches for the Brazilian Under 17 squad, leading many to believe that he was a player of such quality that it might be worth trying him out at a higher level. He was given a Brazilian debut in 1994 against Argentina and was part of the squad that would eventually go on to win the World Cup in America, although Ronaldo did not play and would have to eventually wait eight years before fulfilling his own destiny as far as the World Cup was concerned.

At the end of the competition Ronaldo was sold to Dutch club PSV Eindhoven, helping the club win the Dutch Cup during his two years in Holland. It was his spell at PSV that Ronaldo would later claim that contained his happiest memories, with the roles played by manager Bobby Robson and Director of Football Frank Arnesen key to his development. In 1996 he was sold on to Barcelona, scoring 34 goals in 37 appearances and helping the club win the European Cup Winners' Cup with a 1-0 win over holders Paris Saint-Germain.

At the end of the season Ronaldo was off again, sold to Inter Milan and would help his new club win the UEFA Cup at the end of his first campaign. By then Ronaldo had twice been acclaimed as World Player of the Year (1996 and 1997) and was a key member of the Brazilian side that would attempt to defend their World Cup title in France.

Although he did not set the competition alight in the early stages, Ronaldo did still manage four goals to help Brazil reach the final, but the night before what should have been the biggest game of his life,

BELOW
Ronaldo celebrates scoring for Brazil against Chile in the 1998 World Cup.

Ronaldo suffered a mysterious fit and was rushed to hospital. Such was his state of mind at the time, the manager announced his side to face France in the final, with Ronaldo's name omitted. According to some reports, Ronaldo was reinstated into the side on the instructions of the sponsors, but it was obvious throughout the match that Ronaldo was little more than a passenger. Robbed of any meaningful contribution from their striker, Brazil slumped to a 3-0 defeat.

That was to be the start of almost four years of unrelenting misery for Ronaldo. A badly injured right knee sidelined him for several months and on his return he lasted just seven minutes before breaking down during a match against Lazio. It was to take two operations and almost twenty months before Ronaldo re-appeared, but fortunately for him he had enough time to prove his fitness just before the 2002 World Cup kicked off. Brazil reached the final once again, and this time it was a razor sharp Ronaldo that was on display, plundering the two goals that won the trophy.

If his international career had been resurrected, the same could not be said for his domestic career, for Ronaldo had frequent run-ins with Inter Milan coach Hector Cuper and eventually a move away from the club was deemed to be in everyone's best interests. A £27 million move to the Galactico's of Real Madrid was subsequently arranged and at the end of the season Ronaldo finally achieved something that had eluded him in his League career up to that point – he helped Real Madrid win La Liga.

LEFT
Ronaldo playing for
Real Madrid in 2005.

FAR LEFT
Ronaldo scores for
Brazil in 2004, against
Bolivia in a South
American World
Cup qualifier.

BELOW
Ronaldo with the
European Cup
Winners' Cup, which
he helped Barcelona
win in 1997.

That, unfortunately, remains the only time Ronaldo
has tasted League Championship success, for the
exploits of his compatriot Ronaldinho at his former club
Barcelona have over shadowed almost everything Real
Madrid has done since that title. Success in Europe has
proved elusive, the title almost impossible to wrest away
from Barcelona; Real Madrid coaches have lost their jobs
and at times the fans have turned on their heroes, with
Ronaldo and his fluctuating weight being a regular target
for the boo boys.

Ronaldo has seen it before, however and returned to
sharpness and form when it really matters. Both could
be needed if Brazil are to lift the World Cup again in the
summer of 2006; Ronaldinho may give them the flair,
but a fully committed Ronaldo virtually guarantees
them the goals.

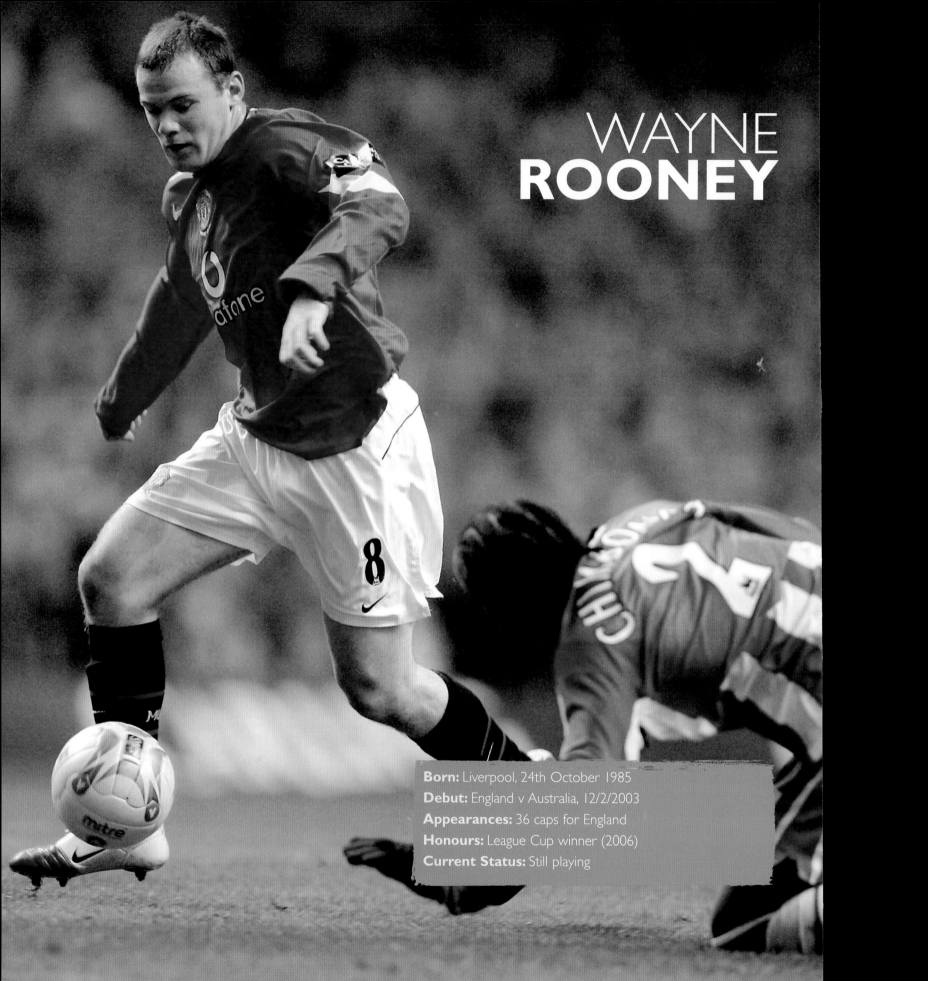

WAYNE
ROONEY

Born: Liverpool, 24th October 1985
Debut: England v Australia, 12/2/2003
Appearances: 36 caps for England
Honours: League Cup winner (2006)
Current Status: Still playing

It is a claim that is made for virtually every young player who bursts onto the scene and makes an initial impact – there is no limit to what this player can achieve. Many fall by the wayside, burnt out or overburdened by the weight of expectation, but the same cannot be said for **Wayne Rooney** – the youngest ever England international, the youngest ever England goalscorer, holder of 30 caps by the time he was twenty and with 11 goals to his credit – an injury free career could see him go on to beat both Peter Shilton's appearance record (125 caps) and Bobby Charlton's goal tally (49 goals) by the time he finally hangs up his boots.

Born in Liverpool in 1985 Wayne was an Everton supporter (as was his entire family) as a boy and made his first appearance for the club as a match day mascot against Liverpool. His exploits in the streets, kicking a ball virtually all the time soon had Everton signing him as a trainee, with Wayne soon breaking into the youth side and becoming a player of considerable promise. He fulfilled that early promise too, helping the youth team reach the final of the FA Youth Cup in 2002, although they had to settle for a runners-up spot after an aggregate defeat by Aston Villa.

Later the same year Wayne became the youngest player to appear in a first team match for Everton and noted the occasion with a stunning goal against Arsenal, a goal that enabled him to become the youngest scorer at the age of just 16 years and 360 days. Four months later he became the youngest player to have earned full international recognition from England, being 17 years and 111 days

when brought on to replace Paul Scholes in the friendly against Australia. One hundred and six days later he became the country's youngest ever goalscorer, netting England's first goal in the 2-1 away win over Macedonia in the European Championship qualifier.

He scored next time out too, England's second in the 2-0 win over Liechenstein, but it was his performance in the vital qualifier away in Istanbul against Turkey that made his reputation. Although the match was played out with an air of hostility towards the England team hanging over the stadium throughout, Wayne was not alone in displaying a cool and collected performance, although when matters did explode, supposedly in the tunnel as the team's left the field at half time, Wayne was one of the first to rush to the assistance of a team mate.

His performances during the finals in Portugal had him marked as one of the true greats in the making. Two goals against Switzerland and again against Croatia put England into the quarter-finals and seemingly on

BELOW

Rooney celebrates scoring for Manchester United, his team's fourth goal during the Carling Cup Final between Wigan Athletic at the Millennium Stadium Wales, 2006.

their way to lifting the trophy. Although England scored first against hosts Portugal, through Michael Owen, an unfortunate injury to Wayne as he bore down on goal left him with a broken metatarsal in his foot and out of not only the competition but out of the game for a considerable time.

Whilst he sat out the rest of the competition, his stock had risen during the European Championships and he returned home considered a hero but with much speculation concerning his future. Whilst Everton were hopeful of keeping him at the club, going as far to slapping a £50 million fee on his head, others were convinced he could be prised away for considerably less. In the end they were right, Everton accepting a fee believed to be £20 million from Manchester United, along with further guarantees and bonuses of a further £5 million depending on future success.

The deal was completed whilst Wayne was still on the road to recovery, finally making his bow for the club in the European Champions League match against Fenerbahce and marking the occasion by scoring a hat-trick. Those were to be the only goals he scored in European football that season, although he did net eleven in the League and four in the FA Cup as United finished third in the League and runners-up in the cup. Despite United's penalty shoot out defeat by Arsenal, Wayne did enough to earn the Man of the Match award on the day.

Rooney on the pitch could deliver the greatest honours imaginable, whilst a distracted Wayne Rooney off it could fall into the same temptations that bedevilled George Best and Paul Gascoigne.

Thus the next few years promise to be interesting ones for Wayne Rooney, Manchester United and England. Is he to be another who promised much but delivered little, or is he genuinely a legend in the making? Only time, and Wayne Rooney, can tell.

LEFT
Rooney evades Maximiliano Rodriguez of Argentina during their international friendly match, November 2005.

FAR LEFT
Rooney in action for Everton, 2002.

BELOW
Man of the Match Wayne Rooney, February 2006.

The following season was another one of disappointment for United, at least as far as their own high expectancy levels were concerned, with the club having to settle for victory in the League Cup as some consolation after disappointments in the League, FA Cup and Europe. Wayne Rooney did not mind – it enabled him to collect the first major winners' medal of his career.

Whilst Wayne is undoubtedly a headline writers dream for his abilities on the field, his exploits off it have also seen him court controversy during his short career. It is this aspect of his temperament and personality that the management teams at both club and country level are working hard to control or change as appropriate – a fully committed Wayne

PAOLO**ROSS**

According to many Italians, Paolo Rossi virtually single-handedly won the 1982 World Cup for Italy, taking them past the Brazilians in the final second-group stage and overcoming the West Germans in the final. His exploits earned him just about every plaudit and award that was going and completed one of the biggest turnarounds in football history, for some two years previously, Paolo had been banned from the game for three years after being caught up in a fixing scandal!

Born in Santa Lucia he was spotted by Juventus and joined the club as a junior, but a series of knee injuries, which required a total of three operations before he'd even made a first-team appearance, saw him sent on loan to first Como and then Lanerossi Vicenza. At the time of joining Vicenza he was playing as a winger, but for some reason Vicenza thought he might be better employed in the opponents' penalty area than out on the wing and converted him to centre forward. It was to be a move that resulted in his career taking a definite turn for the better.

His 21 goals in Serie B helped Vicenza win promotion to the top flight and a grateful club paid Juventus £1.5 million to sign him permanently. Unfortunately both Vicenza and Paolo found life in the higher division a step too much and the club was relegated back almost immediately. Rossi was placed on the transfer list with a £3 million fee on his head, with Napoli making enquiries about signing him. Paolo refused to join the Naples club, however, and was instead sent on loan to Perugia. It was here he became embroiled in the match fixing scandal that was seemingly to end his career, for after netting both of Perugia's goals in their 2-2 draw with Avellino in 1980, accusations that the match had been fixed began to surface and Paolo Rossi was held to be one of the players involved and handed a three-year ban from the game. Paolo protested his innocence, so much so that the ban was eventually reduced to two years, and even though he was suspended, Juventus paid £500,000 in 1981 to take him to Turin.

He returned to action just in time to stake a claim for the Italian World Cup squad for the 1982 competition in Spain, with coach Enzo Bearzot claiming that despite his enforced absence he was still one of the best predators inside the penalty area he had seen,

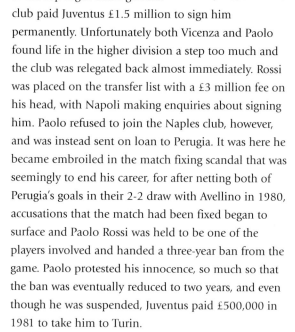

Born: Santa Lucia, 23rd September, 1956

Debut: Belgium v Italy, 21/12/1977

Appearances: 48 caps for Italy

Honours: World Cup winner (1982), UEFA Cup winner (1984), European Cup winner (1985), European Super Cup winner (1984), Intercontinental Cup winner (1985), Italian champions (1984, 1986), Italian Cup winner (1983), European Footballer of the Year (1982), World Player of the Year (1982)

Current Status: Retired

Legends of **FOOTBALL**

competition, a remarkable return for a player who had spent the previous two years watching from the sidelines.

Paolo was also able to repay Juventus for their faith in him, helping them win the Italian Cup in 1983, the UEFA Cup and Italian League in 1984 and the European Cup in 1985, although this latter victory was somewhat tainted by the events that unfolded at the Heysel Stadium that evening.

After helping Juventus to another League title in 1986 Paolo journeyed to Mexico to try and help Italy retain the World Cup but he was as out of sorts with the heat and altitude as his team-mates and they went out in the second round. Paolo then moved on to AC Milan, earning the affection of his club's supporters with a two-goal display against bitter rivals Inter, and then had a brief spell with Verona before retiring in 1987. When his playing career came to an end he became a property developer.

qualities he had displayed during the previous World Cup campaign in Argentina.

In his opening matches Paolo found the pace beyond him, but he was not alone as Italy stumbled along in the competition, qualifying out of the group stages without winning a match and entering a second group that contained World champions Argentina and favourites Brazil. Stirred into life, Italy effectively knocked the Argentineans out of the competition with a 2-1 victory in their first match. When Brazil completed the job with a 3-1 victory, it meant Brazil needed only a draw to qualify for the semi-finals; Italy had to win. Paolo Rossi was restored to the starting line up and proved every one of Enzo Beazot's words correct; every time Brazil thought they had got the goals they needed to qualify, Paolo Rossi would pop up in their penalty area to peg them back. He grabbed a hat-trick in the 3-2 win, a result that proved that Italy could attack with the best of them when required. Paolo was at it again in the semi-final, netting both Italy's goals in the 2-0 win over Poland to earn a place in the final. He then opened the scoring in the final itself, setting Italy on the way to an unlikely 3-1 win to claim their third World Cup. His six goals enabled him to finish top scorer in the

MARCO**VANBASTEN**

Born: Utrecht, 31st October 1964

Debut: Holland v Iceland, 7/9/1983

Appearances: 58 caps for Holland

Honours: Dutch Champions (1982, 1983, 1985), Dutch Cup winners (1983, 1986, 1987), Italian Champions (1988, 1992, 1993, 1994), European Cup winners (1989, 1990), European Cup Winners' Cup winners (1987), European Championship winners (1988), European Player of the Year (1988, 1989, 1992), World Player of the Year (1988, 1992), FIFA Player of the Year (1992)

Current Status: Retired

After near misses in the 1974 and 1978 World Cups, Holland languished in the doldrums for the next decade, looking for players of the calibre of Johan Cruyff and Johan Neeskens to revitalise themselves. Players like Cruyff and Neeskens only come along once in a lifetime, but in Ruud Gullit and Marco van Basten, they found them a second time.

Born in Utrecht in 1964, Marco was playing junior football for Elinkwijk when he was spotted by Ajax and snapped up as an eighteen-year-old. Like the national side, Ajax were looking to return to former glories, the memory of their successes in the European Cup in the 1970s diminishing with each passing year. In Marco van Basten, quickly renamed Marco Goalo, San Marco and The Swan of Utrecht, they found the player who could fire them to glory. Two footed, with exceptional close control skills, powerful and quick on the turn as well as masterful in the air, there were little or no flaws in Marco van Basten's game, making him one of the best predator's in front of goal that the Dutch had uncovered in many a year.

Although they were to be Dutch Champions in 1982, 1983 and 1985, it was in the European Cup Winners Cup that Ajax finally got another taste of European success, lifting the trophy in 1987 with a 1-0 win over Lokomotiv Leipzig. That turned out to be Marco's last match for Ajax, for after scoring 128 goals in just 143 League appearances, he was targeted by an AC Milan club attempting to build a new side of their own.

A total of £20 million was spent acquiring Marco van Basten, Ruud Gullit and Frank Rijkaard, money that proved well spent when the three

Dutchmen turned their new club into Italian Champions at the end of their first season, even though Marco played only eleven games owing to injury. Twelve months later the European Cup was delivered, with Marco scoring two of the goals in the 4-0 victory over Steau Bucharest in Barcelona. AC Milan retained the trophy the following year, this time with a 1-0 win over Benfica.

By then Marco had also delivered success on the international stage, with Holland winning the European Championship in 1988 in Germany. Ruud Gullit may have got more of the plaudits, but Marco van Basten got most of the goals, including the goal of the tournament, a volley from an acute angle in the final against Russia that secured the 2-0 win having earlier netted a hat-trick against England.

Unfortunately that was as good as it got at international level for Marco and his team-mates, for the next few major tournaments saw them invariably installed as pre-competition

BELOW
Marco van Basten runs with the ball during a Holland v Egypt game at the 1990 World Cup.

favourites and then fall short when it mattered.

At club level there was continued success for Marco to enjoy, including three consecutive League titles and a further appearance in the European Cup final, one which initially resulted in a victory for Marseille, only for the French side to be stripped of their title after it was revealed they had bribed a side in a League match. Whilst AC Milan were winning silverware on the field, Marco van Basten was collecting it off the field, including European Player of the Year on three occasions, World Player of the Year twice and FIFA World Player of the Year in 1992.

All of these awards came with a price however, for an ankle injury Marco had suffered during his time at Ajax started to give him further trouble, requiring numerous operations to try and heal the problem. Not all of these were successful, prompting Marco to comment that 'The person who damaged my ankle the most was not a player but a surgeon.'

His last international appearance had come in October 1992 in a World Cup qualifier against Poland, his 58 appearances having brought him 24 goals. His last competitive match for AC Milan came in that infamous European final against Marseille, although the club was to return to the final once again, this time winning the trophy in 1994 with a 4-0 victory over Barcelona. Ultimately Marco van Basten accepted the inevitable and announced his retirement in August

MARCO**VANBASTEN**

would know, having suffered more than almost any other striker of his era.

After leaving AC Milan Marco stated he would never go into management but, like many others, found he needed to be involved in the game in any capacity and so took a coaching course with the Royal Netherlands Football Association. He then moved on to Ajax to coach the reserve side and, in July 2004, was appointed national coach.

1995, having scored 90 goals in 147 appearances for AC Milan.

Despite his admission that his retirement was as much down to surgery as robust defending, Marco was always an advocate for making the striker's life a little easier. He put forward the view that football could learn from other sports, such as basketball, and introduce a personal foul rule, whereby after five fouls a player has to be substituted, even if none of the fouls were reckless enough to warrant a card. Indeed, Marco said 'I really believe that only red and yellow cards are not enough anymore. Defenders have become so subtle nowadays, that a lot of fouls are disguised.' And Marco

FRITZ**WALTER**

But for the football knowledge and intervention of a Hungarian prison guard, Fritz Walter would not only have been lost to the game of football but would probably have perished in a Russian prisoner of war camp at the end of the Second World War. The intervention was one that Fritz Walter, a modest and unassuming man, never forgot, and when the opportunity arose to repay the favour did so uncomplainingly.

Born in Kaiserlautern in 1920, Fritz joined the local club's youth academy at the age of eight, thus beginning

Born: Kaiserlautern, 31st October 1920
Died: 17th June 2002
Debut: Germany v Romania, 14/7/1940
Appearances: 61 caps for Germany
Honours: World Cup winner (1954), German League champions (1951, 1953)
Current Status: Deceased

an association with the club that would last until his retirement in 1959. With his father an official of the club, there was always going to be only one club that Fritz would initially sign for, but his loyalty through the decades after are almost unrivalled.

He made his first-team debut in 1937 and within three years had made the German national side, making his debut against Romania in Frankfurt in 1940 and scoring a hat-trick in the 9-3 victory. By then the Second World War was in full swing and Germany were effectively confined to fixtures against allies or neutral countries. International football was effectively ended after a match against Slovakia in November 1942, with Fritz being drafted into the Wermacht that same year and seeing action on the Eastern Front.

Fritz was in Hungary when the Second World War came to an end, being held in a prisoner of war camp awaiting either the Russians from the East or Allies from the West to overrun the camp and decide the fate of the

proceeded on to the final after victories over Yugoslavia and Austria. The West Germans, inspired by Fritz Walter and also featuring his brother Ottmar in the same line up recovered from going two goals behind to win 3-2, with the Walters becoming the first brothers to have won winners' medals and Fritz having netted three goals along the way, earning him the moniker Hero of Berne.

Fritz was still a regular in the side that travelled to Sweden in 1958 to defend their trophy, but he suffered an injury in the semi-final defeat against the hosts that ended the German campaign and brought an end to Fritz's international career after 61 appearances and 33 goals. Although he was 42 years of age by the time the 1962 tournament came around and had been retired from all football since 1959, manager Sepp Herberger still tried to convince him to come out of retirement and aid the German cause! Fritz decided against it and West Germany made the quarter-final without him.

In all Fritz made 379 appearances for Kaiserlautern and scored 306 goals, and as well as winning two championships was awarded the Grand Cross of the Order of Merit of the Federal Republic of Germany as well as becoming an Honorary Captain of Germany and FIFA Order of Merit in 1995.

Whilst Fritz had played an integral part in ending the Hungarian hopes in the 1954 World Cup final, he never forgot the debt he owed to Hungary for saving his life at the end of the Second World War – when the Hungarian revolution exploded in 1956, stranding many of their better players in Europe, including Ferenc Puskas, Fritz Walter stepped in to manage the affairs of many of them and helped provide financial backing by which a number of Hungarian players survived over the next couple of years.

The stadium at Kaiserlautern was eventually renamed the Fritz Walter Stadion on his 65th birthday in 1985, thus ensuring lasting recognition for one of the greatest players in German history.

His name has also survived thanks to modern folklore – for many years it was noted that he played better the worse the weather was, so 'Fritz Walter Weather' is used today to describe stormy weather conditions!

LEFT
The German national team of 1954 with Fritz Walter (first left).

inmates. As it was the Russians arrived first, with most of the inmates being carted off to a Russian Gulag where life expectancy was five years at most. A guard at the camp had seen Fritz play for Germany prior to the war, and so when the Russians arrived told them that Fritz Walter was Austrian – this white lie effectively saved him from imprisonment in the East and effectively saved his life.

When Fritz Walter was able to resume his football career he returned to Kaiserlautern, eventually guiding them to national championships in 1951 and 1953. In 1951 he was again selected for international duty by Sepp Herberger, going on to captain the West German side and led them into the 1954 World Cup finals in Switzerland.

With a complicated qualifying procedure in place during the finals, with seeded clubs being kept apart, Herberger fielded a weakened side against the Hungarians, confident that his side could get the better of Turkey in a play-off. This they duly did and restored to full strength for the rest of the competition,

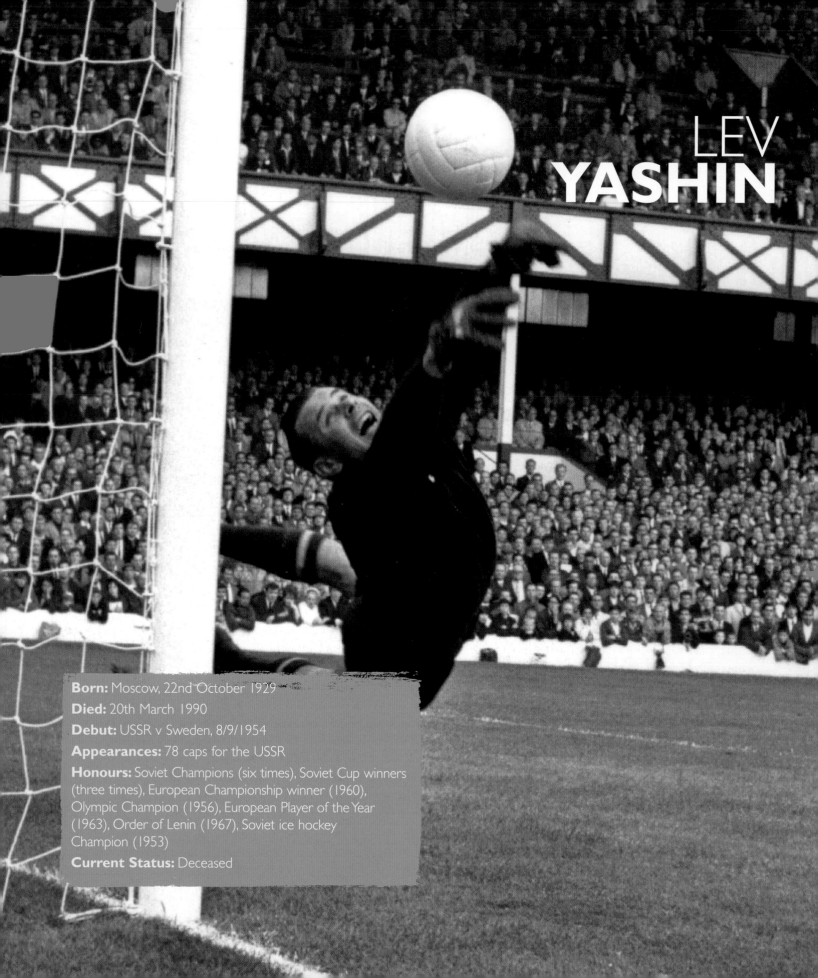

LEV
YASHIN

Born: Moscow, 22nd October 1929

Died: 20th March 1990

Debut: USSR v Sweden, 8/9/1954

Appearances: 78 caps for the USSR

Honours: Soviet Champions (six times), Soviet Cup winners (three times), European Championship winner (1960), Olympic Champion (1956), European Player of the Year (1963), Order of Lenin (1967), Soviet ice hockey Champion (1953)

Current Status: Deceased

Whilst Lev Yashin's exploits as a goalkeeper are known the world over, it is often forgotten how close he came to being lost to football, for after three unsuccessful attempts at breaking into the Moscow Dynamo side, he turned his attentions to ice-hockey and was good enough to help his side win the Soviet Championship at the sport. Not surprisingly, he played as goalkeeper.

Born in Moscow Lev was just twelve when he first went to work, being pressed into vital war duty as a helper in the metal workshops whilst the Germans were laying siege to the city. At the end of the war Lev turned to sport and joined Dynamo Moscow in 1949. He was to spend all of his illustrious career with the club, helping them to six League titles and three cup wins. Like many clubs in Russia, Moscow Dynamo was a multi-sport organisation and Lev's abilities as a goalkeeper on the football field were also utilised by the ice-hockey team and Lev was a member of the side that won the Soviet Championship in 1953.

As mentioned earlier, Lev's chances of progressing in the football side initially looked slim, the continued good form of 'Tiger' Khomich barring the way at both club and national level. Eventually, however, the younger Lev began to make his impact felt, collecting the first of his 74 caps for his country in 1954. Two years later Lev was part of the side that won the Olympic Games in Melbourne, beating Yugoslavia 1-0 in the final.

Lev made his World Cup debut two years later in Sweden, appearing in all five of Russia's matches as they reached the quarter-final, including both matches against England (a group match and then a play-off that Russia ultimately won). By the time the 1962 tournament came around Lev was widely regarded as the greatest goalkeeper in the world, although his reputation took a bit of a battering during the competition, being held at fault during the 4-4 group match with Yugoslavia and the quarter-final defeat at the hands of Chile. The following year Lev restored his reputation with a stunning display during the England versus the Rest of the World at Wembley in a match to celebrate the one hundredth anniversary of the FA, restricting England to just two goals when their attacking play deserved more. He was also named European Player of the Year, the only goalkeeper so honoured.

Three years later Lev was back in England, this time for the 1966 World Cup finals, helping the Russians finish in fourth place. They might have done better too, for Lev conceded only two goals in the run to the semi-final and the team appeared to have a little bit too much

LEFT
Yashin playing for the Soviet Union protects himself after recovering the ball, 1966.

FAR LEFT
Portrait of Yashin voted European Footballer of the Year 1963.

choice and travelled as third goalkeeper, ultimately not being required during the competition.

Lev did get his hands on some silverware during his time as national goalkeeper, helping Russia win the inaugural European Championship in 1960 with a 2-1 victory over Yugoslavia in the final. Four years later they nearly retained the trophy, being beaten by Spain by a similar score in Madrid.

By the time he retired in 1971 he had appeared in 812 first class matches, keeping clean sheets in 480 of them. An imposing sight, standing 6' 3" and usually dressed in all black, he had been known as The Black Panther, Black Spider and Black Octopus during the course of his career. Whatever they called him, they all feared him as an opponent, especially those who faced him in a penalty shoot out – Lev is credited with 150 penalty saves during his career. Asked for the secret of his astonishing success rate, he answered that he would 'have a smoke to calm the nerves, then toss back a strong drink to tone the muscles.' This was probably said tongue very firmly in the cheek, for Lev also once said 'The joy of seeing Yuri Gagarin flying in space is only superseded by the joy of a good penalty save.'

After his retirement FIFA staged a testimonial in his honour in Moscow, with 100,000 fans turning out to see the likes of Pelé, Eusebio and Beckenbauer come along to pay tribute. Lev then went to coach in Finland, working with minor league and youth teams until he was required to have a leg amputated after an earlier knee injury caused him problems. In 1990 further complications set in and he died on 20th March of that year.

experience for the West Germans, but Chislenko's sending off and an injury to another player gave the Russians a hurdle too many to overcome. Lev did accompany the Russian squad to the finals in Mexico in 1970, but by this time he had been replaced as first

His reputation has endured however and in 2000 he was named World Keeper of the Century by FIFA, ahead of the likes of Gordon Banks, a fitting tribute to an exceptional player, no matter what sport he tried his hand at.

ZICO

Regarded as one of the finest midfield talents Brazil ever uncovered, Zico's international career never quite scaled the heights expected, with all three of his World cup campaigns ending in bitter disappointment.

Born in the Rio de Janeiro suburb of Quintino, Zico grew up playing football in the street and dreaming of following his three brothers and father into the professional game. Eventually he came to the attention of radio presenter Celso Garcia who organised a trial with the local Flamengo club. Somewhat frail as a youngster, the club organised a series of body building exercises to build him up and a year later, still aged only 16, handed him a first team debut.

After a brief run out with the first team Zico was sent back to the youth side to continue his development, with a special diet also being set to further build his strength. When he returned a second time to first team duties, it was a more confident and physically stronger Zico that Flamengo fans got to see. He repeated that ability to the international stage too, representing Brazil in the Olympic Games and going on to win his first full cap in 1975.

Brazil's disappointing performance in the 1974 World Cup had seen the entire side dismantled and a new side built in its place, with Zico seen as being the creative midfield influence on the side. That was the role he performed with Flamengo, but new Brazilian coach Claudio Coutinho had other ideas, handing Zico an altogether different role. Zico went with the squad to Argentina for the 1978 World Cup but was in and out of the side as Brazil limped their way through. Zico, and Brazil, were finally let off the leash in the final match against Poland, a match that Brazil had to win in order to advance to the final. Zico was at his imperious best to guide his country to a 3-1 win, but as the Brazil match finished early, Argentina knew a victory in their final match by more than four goals would take them to the final – they won 6-0. Although Brazil wound up the competition with a 2-1 win over Italy for third and fourth place, Zico was once again left out of the side.

By the time the World Cup hit Spain in 1982, Brazil were seen as being almost back to their best, with Zico scoring three of their goals in the first group stage.

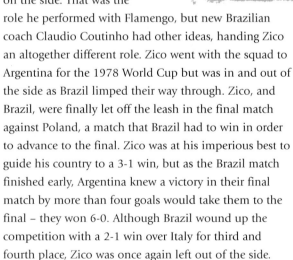

Born: Rio de Janeiro, 3rd March 1953
Debut: Brazil v Uruguay, 25/2/1976
Appearances: 72 caps for Brazil
Honours: Brazilian Champions (1980, 1983, 1987), Copa Libertadores winners (1981), World Player of the Year (1983)
Current Status: Retired

LEFT
Zico takes on a French defender for Brazil during the World Cup, 1986.

BELOW
A portrait of Japan Manager Zico.

and lows. He was an exceptional performer for Flamengo, helping them win two national Championships, six state titles and the South American and World club Championships, hitting 630 goals in the process! Like many of his compatriots he was briefly lured to Europe, joining Udinese for £2.5 million in 1983 and topping the goalscoring charts with 19 goals in his first season. Unfortunately the second season saw him struggle owing to a succession of injuries and he returned to Flamengo in 1985, helping them to another national Championship in 1987. Following the election of Fernando Collor de Mello as President of Brazil, Zico accepted an invitation to become Minister of Sports. He held the post for almost a year, being chiefly responsible for introducing new legislation that dealt with the business organisation of Brazilian sports clubs, most of which were run like amateur associations.

Zico left his ministerial post in 1991 in order to return to football, joining the Japanese club Kashima Antlers in the J League. Here too Zico made his presence felt, turning a small provincial club into one of the best in the country by the time he finally retired from playing in 1994. He was appointed technical adviser of the club and continued to spend his time between Japan and his Brazilian homeland. In 1995 he launched CFZ, the Zico Football Centre in Brazil, an opportunity for one of the best players in the world to give something back to his countrymen.

Victory over Argentina in the next round of matches went some way to burying the ghosts of 1978, but a shock 3-2 defeat at the hands of eventual Champions Italy ended Brazil's interest before the semi-final stage, the first time Brazil had failed to make the semi-finals since 1966.

Zico's final appearance in the World Cup finals came in Mexico in 1986, but by then he was 33 years of age and struggling to overcome a knee injury. He made three substitute appearances, failing to score in any of them, although he did have a chance from the penalty spot soon after coming on against France in the quarter-final but missed. Zico recovered from that mishap to score during the penalty shoot out at the end of the match, but Brazil still went out.

Whilst his international career promised much but delivered little, his club career was a mixture of highs

ZINEDINE
ZIDANE

Born: Marseille, 23rd June 1972

Debut: France v Czech Republic, 17/8/1994

Appearances: 108 caps for France

Honours: World Cup winner (1998), European Championship winner (2000), Italian League champion (1997, 1998), Spanish League champions (2003), UEFA Champions League winner (2002), European Super Cup winner (1996, 2002), Italian Super Cup winner (1997), Spanish Super Cup winner (2001, 2003)

Current Status: Retired

Two headed goals in the 1998 World Cup Final ensured France finally got their hands on the trophy they had been instrumental in instigating and cemented Zinedine Zidane's reputation as perhaps the most complete midfield player of his generation. Different use of the head at the same stage eight years later brought an unceremonious end to his participation in the final and to his career. Could it ever have been any different for such a complex character?

Born in Marseille to Algerian immigrants and the youngest of five children, Zinedine began his footballing career with US Saint-Henri, a local club in the La Castellane district of Marseille. A coach at Saint-Henri then recommended him to Septemes Sports Olympiques, where he would remain until the age of 14. He then joined AS Cannes in 1988, making 61 appearances for the side in four years before switching to FC Girondins de Bordeaux. He began to make a reputation as a quality midfield player, inspiring Bordeaux to victory in the Inter-Toto Cup (there isn't an actual cup to win, but rather entry into the UEFA Cup) in 1995 and propelling then on to runners-up spot in the UEFA Cup later that season.

A €3 million deal took him to Juventus in the summer of 1996, with Zinedine slotting in alongside such luminaries as Didier Deschamps, Allesandro Del Piero and Edgar Davids. This side was of sufficient quality to win the Italian Serie A in 1997 and 1998, but the UEFA Champions League proved just beyond them, finishing runners-up in 1997 and 1998, the latter against Real Madrid.

Just as he was seen as the focal point of the Juventus side, so the French national side was built around his mercurial talents. Having made his debut in 1994 (he holds dual nationality and could therefore have played for Algeria, but the Algerian coach felt he wasn't fast enough), he was an integral part of the side that prepared to try and win the World Cup on home soil in 1998, having already taken them to the semi finals of the European Championship in 1996. Zinedine made an impact of sorts during the group stages, being sent off for stamping on Faud Amin of Saudi Arabia and earning a two-match ban, although Zinedine claimed he had been verbally abused. He came back into the side in time to help them overcome Italy in a penalty shoot out and then scored two of the goals in a 3-0 final win over Brazil.

Two years later he was much more controlled and was little short of inspirational as France powered their way to the final of the European Championships, beating Italy in the final and thus becoming the first side in 34 years to hold both the World Cup and European Championship. His performances for France, as well as Juventus, were envied around the world and only a record-breaking transfer was likely to prise him

away from Italy. Real Madrid stepped in with a €66 million deal in 2001, making Zinedine the most expensive player in the world.

Victory in the UEFA Champions League in 2002 would suggest it was money well spent, and with a winners' medal safely deposited, Zinedine set off to help France defend their World Cup in Japan. He was suffering a thigh injury when the tournament kicked off, resulting in him having to sit on the sidelines as France struggled to make any kind of progress. He was rushed back into the side for the make or break third-group match but was clearly struggling and could do little to prevent France going out of the competition in double quick time. On return to club duty he helped Real Madrid win the Spanish League in 2003, the only League title won during his time with the club.

In 2004 he helped France reach the quarter-finals of the European Championship before being eliminated by the eventual winners Greece. Zinedine then called time on his international career, preferring to concentrate on his club career. However, a disastrous start to the qualifying campaign for the 2006 World Cup led to calls for him to reconsider and in August 2005 he returned to the French side, not just in the team but as captain.

France duly qualified for Germany, although Zinedine suffered a number of injuries along the way. In April 2006 he announced his intention to retire from all football at the end of the season, bringing down the curtain on his club career at the Bernabeu Stadium, helping them to qualify for the UEFA Champions League even if they failed to lift the League title.

Thus the stage was set for Zinedine's career to come to an end on the world stage, appearing in the World Cup. After a stuttering start France moved through the competition, although once again they had to do so without Zinedine, booked in both the opening matches and thus serving a suspension come the third-group match. France made the knockout stage with Zinedine back in the side, scoring in the 3-1 win over Spain, setting up the winner against Brazil and netting the only

agree. Irrespective of what was said, the head butt and sending off (the fourteenth of his career) earned Zinedine a three-match ban, totally irrelevant as he retired after the match any way! Instead he did three days community service.

Despite the controversial end to his career, Zinedine still made headlines for the right reasons during the 2006 World Cup – he was named player of the tournament and was awarded the FIFA World Cup Golden Ball Award!

goal of the game in the semi-final against Portugal from the penalty spot.

Zinedine also scored from the penalty spot in the final against Italy, thus joining a select band of players who have scored in more than one World Cup final, alongside Pelé, Breitner and Vava. Italy eventually equalised and the game went into extra time. Ten minutes from the final whistle Zinedine was involved in an off the ball incident with Marco Materazzi, culminating in the Frenchman headbutting the Italian in the chest. Although the incident was missed by the referee, either the assistant or fourth or fifth official had spotted it and Zinedine was shown a straight red, thus joining an even smaller select band, alongside Rigobert Song, of having been sent off in more than one World Cup competition! Zinedine claimed Materazzi had insulted his family, a charge the Italian did not deny, although the pair differed over what exactly was said. Lip readers were supposedly brought in to try and settle the matter for once and for all but even they could not

DINO**ZOFF**

A European Championship winner at the start of his international career and a World Cup winner near the end, captain of the side that won that World Cup and holder of the record for the longest spell unbeaten by an international goalkeeper, Dino Zoff's career took in all the possible highs, yet he was rejected as a youngster by two clubs who felt he would not be tall enough to be a first class goalkeeper!

Born in Mariano del Friuli in 1942 he had trials as a fourteen-year-old with Inter Milan and Juventus but was turned down by both owing to his height, or rather his lack of it. Five years later and having grown an extra 33 centimetres, Dino was taken on by Udinese and made his debut in Serie A, although after only four appearances he was sold to Mantova in 1963.

At Mantova he was given an extended run in the first team as the side bounced between Serie A and Serie B, although Dino's performances did not go unnoticed by either bigger clubs or the international manager, culminating in Dino being given an international debut in 1968 in the European Championship quarter-final against Bulgaria. He held his place through to the final as Italy overcame Yugoslavia, and thus collected a winners' medal in only his fourth appearance for his country.

Prior to that success Dino had switched clubs to join Napoli, although this was a Napoli side that was struggling to revive their fortunes and could not maintain a challenge for League or cup honours. Dino's international career suffered as a result, for he was left out of the side for the 1970 World Cup in Mexico, where Italy would reach the final before being beaten by Brazil. A move to Juventus in 1972 saw him re-establish his reputation at both club and international level – for Juventus he set a record of 903 minutes unbeaten during the 1972-73 season as Juventus went on to lift the League title, Dino's first domestic success. Restored into the Italian side, he set a world record 1142 minutes without being beaten, a record that stretched across eleven matches from September 1972 to June 1974, with a Haitian striker being responsible for ending the record!

Dino would go on to help Juventus win six League titles during his time with the club, also adding two Italian Cups and the UEFA Cup in that same spell. The

Born: Mariano del Friuli, 28th February 1942

Debut: Italy v Bulgaria, 20/4/1968

Appearances: 112 caps for Italy

Honours: World Cup winner (1982), European Championship winner (1968), UEFA Cup winner (1977), Italian League champion (1973, 1975, 1977, 1978, 1981, 1982), Italian Cup winner (1979, 1983)

Current Status: Retired

Legends of **FOOTBALL**

His international career lasted another year, with Dino finally hanging up his gloves after a 2-0 win over Sweden in May 1983, two weeks after his club career had also come to an end. As well as his 112 international caps, Dino had made 570 appearances in Serie A for his various clubs (then a record) as well as 74 Serie B appearances. In all Dino made 841 first class appearances, including a record 330 consecutive appearances for Juventus.

At the end of his playing career Dino turned to coaching, remaining at Juventus on the technical staff and stepping up to become head coach in 1988, a position he held for two years before being sacked, despite guiding the club to the UEFA Cup in 1990. He then moved on to Lazio and guided the club into the UEFA Cup in 1997, having been appointed club president in 1994.

LEFT
Zoff dives for the ball.

BELOW
Dino Zoff with the World Cup trophy after Italy defeated West Germany 3-1 in the final, 1982.

UEFA Cup success was the only European success he enjoyed, despite saving two penalties in a shoot out against Ajax that took Juventus to the European Cup semi-final in 1978.

After disappointing World Cup campaigns in 1974 (eliminated in the group stage) and 1978 (finished fourth, losing to Brazil again in the play-off), the 1982 World Cup represented a last chance for Dino Zoff. He was captain of the Italian side (he captained the side in 59 of his 112 international appearances) that stumbled their way through the first-group stage (three draws in three matches) and grew in stature thereafter, finally seeing off Brazil in the second-group stage and overcoming Poland to make the final against West Germany. If he was overshadowed on the pitch by the exploits of Paolo Rossi it was only because goalscorers usually get more attention, for Dino put in a masterful performance to enable Italy to win 3-1. As captain, Dino was presented with the trophy, the first goalkeeping captain and the oldest player to have won the World Cup.

In 1998 he was appointed national coach and, despite his former goalkeeping responsibilities got the Italians playing a more open and attacking style which took the side through to the final of the European Championship in 2000. Italy were 1-0 up and less than a minute from winning the trophy when an equaliser took the game into extra time and an eventual French victory. A few days later Dino resigned, stung by some fierce criticism from others within the Italian game. He then resumed his coaching career with Lazio and also had a spell with Fiorentina.

Legends of **FOOTBALL**

THE PICTURES IN THIS BOOK WERE PROVIDED COURTESY OF THE FOLLOWING:

GETTY**IMAGES**
101 Bayham Street, London NW1 0AG

EMPICS
www.empics.com

Concept and Art Direction:
VANESSA **and** KEVIN**GARDNER**

Creative and Artwork: KEVIN**GARDNER**

Image research: ELLIE**CHARLESTON**

PUBLISHED BY GREEN UMBRELLA PUBLISHING

Publishers:
JULES**GAMMOND and** VANESSA**GARDNER**

Written by: GRAHAM**BETTS**